AF271697

THE TRAGEDIE OF JULIUS CAESAR

MJP
PUBLISHERS

THE TRAGEDIE OF JULIUS CAESAR

William Shakespeare

 **MJP** PUBLISHERS

Chennai   New Delhi   Tirunelveli

Honour Copyright
&
Exclude Piracy

This book is protected by copyright. Reproduction of any part in any form including photocopying shall not be done except with authorization from the publisher.

ISBN 978-81-8094-330-0 **MJP Publishers**

All rights reserved No. 44, Nallathambi Street,

Printed and bound in India Triplicane, Chennai 600 005

MJP 301 © Publishers, 2017

Publisher : **C. Janarthanan**

Project Editor : **C. Ambica**

PUBLISHER'S NOTE

The legacy of a country is in its varied cultural heritage, historical literature, developments in the field of economy and science. The top nations in the world are competing in the field of science, economy and literature. This vast legacy has to be conserved and documented so that it can be bestowed to the future generation. The knowledge of this legacy is slowly getting perished in the present generation due to lack of documentation.

Keeping this in mind, the concern with retrospective acquiring of rare books has been accented recently by the burgeoning reprint industry. MJP Publishers is gratified to retrieve the rare collections with a view to bring back those books that were landmarks in their time.

In this effort, a series of rare books would be republished under the banner, "MJP Publishers". The books in the reprint series have been carefully selected for their contemporary usefulness as well as their historical importance within the intellectual. We reconstruct the book with slight enhancements made for better presentation, without affecting the contents of the original edition.

Most of the works selected for republishing covers a huge range of subjects, from history to anthropology. We believe this reprint edition will be a service to the numerous researchers and practitioners active in this fascinating field. We allow readers to experience the wonder of peering into a scholarly work of the highest order and seminal significance.

MJP PUBLISHERS

CONTENTS

Actus Primus

Scoena Prima

Enter Flauius, Murellus, and certaine Commoners ouer the Stage.

Flauius: Hence: home you idle Creatures, get you home:

Is this a Holiday? What, know you not

(Being Mechanicall) you ought not walke

Vpon a labouring day, without the signe

Of your Profession? Speake, what Trade art thou?

Car: Why Sir, a Carpenter

Mur: Where is thy Leather Apron, and thy Rule?

What dost thou with thy best Apparrell on?

You sir, what Trade are you?

Cobl: Truely Sir, in respect of a fine Workman, I am but as you would say, a Cobler

Mur: But what Trade art thou? Answer me directly

Cob: A Trade Sir, that I hope I may vse, with a safe Conscience, which is indeed Sir, a Mender of bad soules

Fla: What Trade thou knaue? Thou naughty knaue, what Trade?

Cobl: Nay I beseech you Sir, be not out with me: yet if you be out Sir, I can mend you

Mur: What mean›st thou by that? Mend mee, thou sawcy Fellow?

Cob: Why sir, Cobble you

Fla: Thou art a Cobler, art thou? Cob. Truly sir, all that I liue by, is with the Aule: I meddle with no Tradesmans matters, nor womens matters; but withal I am indeed Sir, a Surgeon to old shooes: when they are in great danger, I recouer them. As proper men as euer trod vpon Neats Leather, haue gone vpon my handy-worke

Fla: But wherefore art not in thy Shop to day? Why do'st thou leade these men about the streets? Cob. Truly sir, to weare out their shooes, to get my selfe into more worke. But indeede sir, we make Holyday to see Caesar, and to reioyce in his Triumph

Mur: Wherefore reioyce?

What Conquest brings he home?

What Tributaries follow him to Rome,

To grace in Captiue bonds his Chariot Wheeles?

You Blockes, you stones, you worse then sens-lesse things:

O you hard hearts, you cruell men of Rome,

Knew you not Pompey many a time and oft?

Haue you climb'd vp to Walles and Battlements,

To Towres and Windowes? Yea, to Chimney tops,

Your Infants in your Armes, and there haue sate

The liue-long day, with patient expectation,

To see great Pompey passe the streets of Rome:

And when you saw his Chariot but appeare,

Haue you not made an Vniuersall shout,

That Tyber trembled vnderneath her bankes

To heare the replication of your sounds,

Made in her Concaue Shores?

And do you now put on your best attyre?

And do you now cull out a Holyday?

And do you now strew Flowers in his way,

That comes in Triumph ouer Pompeyes blood?

Be gone,

Runne to your houses, fall vpon your knees,

Pray to the Gods to intermit the plague

That needs must light on this Ingratitude

Fla: Go, go, good Countrymen, and for this fault

Assemble all the poore men of your sort;

Draw them to Tyber bankes, and weepe your teares

Into the Channell, till the lowest streame

Do kisse the most exalted Shores of all.

Exeunt. All the Commoners.

See where their basest mettle be not mou'd,

They vanish tongue-tyed in their guiltinesse:

Go you downe that way towards the Capitoll,

This way will I: Disrobe the Images,

If you do finde them deckt with Ceremonies

Mur: May we do so?

        You know it is the Feast of Lupercall

Fla: It is no matter, let no Images

        Be hung with Caesars Trophees: Ile about,

        And driue away the Vulgar from the streets;

        So do you too, where you perceiue them thicke.

        These growing Feathers, pluckt from Caesars wing,

        Will make him flye an ordinary pitch,

        Who else would soare aboue the view of men,

        And keepe vs all in seruile fearefulnesse.

Exeunt.

Enter Caesar, Antony for the Course, Calphurnia, Portia, Decius, Cicero, Brutus, Cassius, Caska, a Soothsayer: after them Murellus and Flauius.

Caes: Calphurnia

Cask: Peace ho, Caesar speakes

Caes: Calphurnia

Calp: Heere my Lord

Caes: Stand you directly in Antonio›s way,

        When he doth run his course. Antonio

Ant: César, my Lord

Caes:	Forget not in your speed Antonio,
	To touch Calphurnia: for our Elders say,
	The Barren touched in this holy chace,
	Shake off their sterrile curse
Ant:	I shall remember,
	When Caesar sayes, Do this; it is perform'd
Caes:	Set on, and leaue no Ceremony out
Sooth:	Caesar
Caes:	Ha? Who calles?
Cask:	Bid euery noyse be still: peace yet againe
Caes:	Who is it in the presse, that calles on me?
	I heare a Tongue shriller then all the Musicke
	Cry, Caesar: Speake, Caesar is turn'd to heare
Sooth:	Beware the Ides of March
Caes:	What man is that?
Br:	A Sooth-sayer bids you beware the Ides of March
Caes:	Set him before me, let me see his face
Cassi:	Fellow, come from the throng, look vpon Caesar
Caes:	What sayst thou to me now? Speak once againe,
Sooth:	Beware the Ides of March
Caes:	He is a Dreamer, let vs leaue him: Passe.
	Sennet

Exeunt. Manet Brut. & Cass.

Cassi:	Will you go see the order of the course?
Brut:	Not I

Cassi: I pray you do

Brut: I am not Gamesom: I do lacke some part

Of that quicke Spirit that is in Antony:

Let me not hinder Cassius your desires;

Ile leaue you

Cassi: Brutus, I do obserue you now of late:

I haue not from your eyes, that gentlenesse

And shew of Loue, as I was wont to haue:

You beare too stubborne, and too strange a hand

Ouer your Friend, that loues you

Bru: Cassius,

Be not deceiu'd: If I haue veyl'd my looke,

I turne the trouble of my Countenance

Meerely vpon my selfe. Vexed I am

Of late, with passions of some difference,

Conceptions onely proper to my selfe,

Which giue some soyle (perhaps) to my Behau-
iours:

But let not therefore my good Friends be greeu'd

(Among which number Cassius be you one)

Nor construe any further my neglect,

Then that poore Brutus with himselfe at warre,

Forgets the shewes of Loue to other men

Cassi: Then Brutus, I haue much mistook your passion,

By meanes whereof, this Brest of mine hath
buried

Thoughts of great value, worthy Cogitations.

Tell me good Brutus, Can you see your face?

Brutus: No Cassius:

For the eye sees not it selfe but by reflection,

By some other things

Cassius: 'Tis iust,

And it is very much lamented Brutus,

That you haue no such Mirrors, as will turne

Your hidden worthinesse into your eye,

That you might see your shadow:

I haue heard,

Where many of the best respect in Rome,

(Except immortall Caesar) speaking of Brutus,

And groaning vnderneath this Ages yoake,

Haue wish'd, that Noble Brutus had his eyes

Bru: Into what dangers, would you

Leade me Cassius?

That you would haue me seeke into my selfe,

For that which is not in me?

Cas: Therefore good Brutus, be prepar'd to heare:

And since you know, you cannot see your selfe

So well as by Reflection; I your Glasse,

Will modestly discouer to your selfe

That of your selfe, which you yet know not of.

And be not iealous on me, gentle Brutus:

Were I a common Laughter, or did vse

To stale with ordinary Oathes my loue

To euery new Protester: if you know,

That I do fawne on men, and hugge them hard,

And after scandall them: Or if you know,

That I professe my selfe in Banquetting

To all the Rout, then hold me dangerous.

Flourish, and Shout.

Bru:	What meanes this Showting?

I do feare, the People choose Caesar

For their King

Cassi:	I, do you feare it?

Then must I thinke you would not haue it so

Bru:	I would not Cassius, yet I loue him well:

But wherefore do you hold me heere so long?

What is it, that you would impart to me?

If it be ought toward the generall good,

Set Honor in one eye, and Death i'th other,

And I will looke on both indifferently:

For let the Gods so speed mee, as I loue

The name of Honor, more then I feare death

Cassi:	I know that vertue to be in you Brutus,

As well as I do know your outward fauour.

Well, Honor is the subiect of my Story:

I cannot tell, what you and other men

Thinke of this life: But for my single selfe,

I had as liefe not be, as liue to be

In awe of such a Thing, as I my selfe.

I was borne free as Caesar, so were you,

We both haue fed as well, and we can both

Endure the Winters cold, as well as hee.

For once, vpon a Rawe and Gustie day,

The troubled Tyber, chafing with her Shores,

Caesar saide to me, Dar'st thou Cassius now

Leape in with me into this angry Flood,

And swim to yonder Point? Vpon the word,

Accoutred as I was, I plunged in,

And bad him follow: so indeed he did.

The Torrent roar'd, and we did buffet it

With lusty Sinewes, throwing it aside,

And stemming it with hearts of Controuersie.

But ere we could arriue the Point propos'd,

Caesar cride, Helpe me Cassius, or I sinke.

I (as Aeneas, our great Ancestor,

Did from the Flames of Troy, vpon his shoulder

The old Anchyses beare) so, from the waues of
Tyber

Did I the tyred Caesar: And this Man,

Is now become a God, and Cassius is

A wretched Creature, and must bend his body,

If Caesar carelesly but nod on him.

He had a Feauer when he was in Spaine,

And when the Fit was on him, I did marke

How he did shake: Tis true, this God did shake,

His Coward lippes did from their colour flye,

And that same Eye, whose bend doth awe the World,

Did loose his Lustre: I did heare him grone:

I, and that Tongue of his, that bad the Romans

Marke him, and write his Speeches in their Bookes,

Alas, it cried, Giue me some drinke Titinius,

As a sicke Girle: Ye Gods, it doth amaze me,

A man of such a feeble temper should

So get the start of the Maiesticke world,

And beare the Palme alone.

Shout. Flourish.

Bru: Another generall shout?

I do beleeue, that these applauses are

For some new Honors, that are heap'd on Caesar

Cassi: Why man, he doth bestride the narrow world

Like a Colossus, and we petty men

Walke vnder his huge legges, and peepe about

To finde our selues dishonourable Graues.

Men at sometime, are Masters of their Fates.

The fault (deere Brutus) is not in our Starres,

But in our Selues, that we are vnderlings.

Brutus and Caesar: What should be in that Caesar?

Why should that name be sounded more then
yours

Write them together: Yours, is as faire a Name:

Sound them, it doth become the mouth aswell:

Weigh them, it is as heauy: Coniure with 'em,

Brutus will start a Spirit as soone as Caesar.

Now in the names of all the Gods at once,

Vpon what meate doth this our Caesar feede,

That he is growne so great? Age, thou art sh-
am'd.

Rome, thou hast lost the breed of Noble Bloods.

When went there by an Age, since the great
Flood,

But it was fam'd with more then with one man?

When could they say (till now) that talk'd of
Rome,

That her wide Walkes incompast but one man?

Now is it Rome indeed, and Roome enough

When there is in it but one onely man.

O! you and I, haue heard our Fathers say,

There was a Brutus once, that would haue
brook'd

Th' eternall Diuell to keepe his State in Rome,

As easily as a King

Bru: That you do loue me, I am nothing iealous:

What you would worke me too, I haue some ayme:

How I haue thought of this, and of these times

I shall recount heereafter. For this present,

I would not so (with loue I might intreat you)

Be any further moou'd: What you haue said,

I will consider: what you haue to say

I will with patience heare, and finde a time

Both meete to heare, and answer such high things.

Till then, my Noble Friend, chew vpon this:

Brutus had rather be a Villager,

Then to repute himselfe a Sonne of Rome

Vnder these hard Conditions, as this time

Is like to lay vpon vs

Cassi: I am glad that my weake words

Haue strucke but thus much shew of fire from Brutus,

Enter Caesar and his Traine.

Bru: The Games are done,

And Caesar is returning

Cassi: As they passe by,

Plucke Caska by the Sleeue,

And he will (after his sowre fashion) tell you

What hath proceeded worthy note to day

Bru: I will do so: but looke you Cassius,

The angry spot doth glow on Caesars brow,

And all the rest, looke like a chidden Traine;

Calphurnia's Cheeke is pale, and Cicero

Lookes with such Ferret, and such fiery eyes

As we haue seene him in the Capitoll

Being crost in Conference, by some Senators

Cassi: Caska will tell vs what the matter is

Caes Antonio

Ant: Caesar

Caes Let me haue men about me, that are fat,

Sleeke-headed men, and such as sleepe a-nights:

Yond Cassius has a leane and hungry looke,

He thinkes too much: such men are dangerous

Ant: Feare him not Caesar, he›s not dangerous,

He is a Noble Roman, and well giuen

Caes Would he were fatter; But I feare him not:

Yet if my name were lyable to feare,

I do not know the man I should auoyd

So soone as that spare Cassius. He reades much,

He is a great Obseruer, and he lookes

Quite through the Deeds of men. He loues no Playes,

As thou dost Antony: he heares no Musicke;

Seldome he smiles, and smiles in such a sort

As if he mock'd himselfe, and scorn'd his spirit

That could be mou'd to smile at any thing.

Such men as he, be neuer at hearts ease,

Whiles they behold a greater then themselues,

And therefore are they very dangerous.

I rather tell thee what is to be fear'd,

Then what I feare: for alwayes I am Caesar.

Come on my right hand, for this eare is deafe,

And tell me truely, what thou think'st of him.

Sennit.

Exeunt. Caesar and his Traine.

Cask:	You pul›d me by the cloake, would you speake with me?
Bru:	I Caska, tell vs what hath chanc'd to day That Caesar lookes so sad
Cask:	Why you were with him, were you not?
Bru:	I should not then aske Caska what had chanc'd
Cask:	Why there was a Crowne offer'd him; & being offer'd him, he put it by with the backe of his hand thus, and then the people fell a shouting
Bru:	What was the second noyse for?
Cask:	Why for that too
Cassi:	They shouted thrice: what was the last cry for?

Cassi: To what effect?

Cask: Nay, and I tell you that, Ile ne're looke you i'th'
          face againe. But those that vnderstood him,
          smil'd at one another, and shooke their heads:
          but for mine owne part, it was Greeke to me.
          I could tell you more newes too: Murrellus and
          Flauius, for pulling Scarffes off Caesars Imag-
          es, are put to silence. Fare you well. There was
          more Foolerie yet, if I could remember it

Cassi: Will you suppe with me to Night, Caska?

Cask: No, I am promis'd forth

Cassi: Will you Dine with me to morrow?

Cask: I, if I be aliue, and your minde hold, and your
          Dinner worth the eating

Cassi: Good, I will expect you

Cask: Doe so: farewell both.

Enter.

Brut: What a blunt fellow is this growne to be?

          He was quick Mettle, when he went to Schoole

Cassi: So is he now, in execution

          Of any bold, or Noble Enterprize,

          How-euer he puts on this tardie forme:

          This Rudenesse is a Sawce to his good Wit,

          Which giues men stomacke to disgest his words

          With better Appetite

Brut: And so it is:

For this time I will leaue you:

To morrow, if you please to speake with me,

I will come home to you: or if you will,

Come home to me, and I will wait for you

Cassi: I will doe so: till then, thinke of the World.

Exit Brutus.

Well Brutus, thou art Noble: yet I see,

Thy Honorable Mettle may be wrought

From that it is dispos'd: therefore it is meet,

That Noble mindes keepe euer with their likes:

For who so firme, that cannot be seduc'd?

Caesar doth beare me hard, but he loues Brutus.

If I were Brutus now, and he were Cassius,

He should not humor me. I will this Night,

In seuerall Hands, in at his Windowes throw,

As if they came from seuerall Citizens,

Writings, all tending to the great opinion

That Rome holds of his Name: wherein obscurely

Caesars Ambition shall be glanced at.

And after this, let Caesar seat him sure,

For wee will shake him, or worse dayes endure.

Enter.

Thunder, and Lightning. Enter Caska, and Cicero.

Cic: Good euen, Caska: brought you Caesar home?

Why are you breathlesse, and why stare you so?

Cask: Are not you mou'd, when all the sway of Earth
Shakes, like a thing vnfirme?

O Cicero,

I haue seene Tempests, when the scolding
Winds

Haue riu'd the knottie Oakes, and I haue seene

Th' ambitious Ocean swell, and rage, and foame,

To be exalted with the threatning Clouds:

But neuer till to Night, neuer till now,

Did I goe through a Tempest-dropping-fire.

Eyther there is a Ciuill strife in Heauen,

Or else the World, too sawcie with the Gods,

Incenses them to send destruction

Cic: Why, saw you any thing more wonderfull?

Cask: A common slaue, you know him well by sight,

Held vp his left Hand, which did flame and burne

Like twentie Torches ioyn'd; and yet his Hand,

Not sensible of fire, remain'd vnscorch'd.

Besides, I ha' not since put vp my Sword,

Against the Capitoll I met a Lyon,

Who glaz'd vpon me, and went surly by,

Without annoying me. And there were drawne

Vpon a heape, a hundred gastly Women,

Transformed with their feare, who swore, they saw

Men, all in fire, walke vp and downe the streetes.

And yesterday, the Bird of Night did sit,

Euen at Noone-day, vpon the Market place,

Howting, and shreeking. When these Prodigies

Doe so conioyntly meet, let not men say,

These are their Reasons, they are Naturall:

For I beleeue, they are portentous things

Vnto the Clymate, that they point vpon

Cic: Indeed, it is a strange disposed time:

But men may construe things after their fashion,

Cleane from the purpose of the things themselues.

Comes Caesar to the Capitoll to morrow?

Cask: He doth: for he did bid Antonio

Send word to you, he would be there to morrow

Cic: Good-night then,

Caska: This disturbed Skie is not to walke in

Cask: Farewell Cicero.

Exit Cicero.

Enter Cassius.

Cassi: Who›s there?

Cask: A Romane

Cassi:	Caska, by your Voyce
Cask:	Your Eare is good.
	Cassius, what Night is this?
Cassi:	A very pleasing Night to honest men
Cask:	Who euer knew the Heauens menace so?
Cassi:	Those that haue knowne the Earth so full of faults.
	For my part, I haue walk'd about the streets,
	Submitting me vnto the perillous Night;
	And thus vnbraced, Caska, as you see,
	Haue bar'd my Bosome to the Thunder-stone:
	And when the crosse blew Lightning seem'd to open
	The Brest of Heauen, I did present my selfe
Cask:	But wherefore did you so much tempt the Heauens?
	It is the part of men, to feare and tremble,
	When the most mightie Gods, by tokens send
	Such dreadfull Heraulds, to astonish vs
Cassi:	You are dull, Caska:
	And those sparkes of Life, that should be in a Roman,
	You doe want, or else you vse not.
	You looke pale, and gaze, and put on feare,
	And cast your selfe in wonder,
	To see the strange impatience of the Heauens:

But if you would consider the true cause,

Why all these Fires, why all these gliding Ghosts,

Why Birds and Beasts, from qualitie and kinde,

Why Old men, Fooles, and Children calculate,

Why all these things change from their Ordinance,

Their Natures, and pre-formed Faculties,

To monstrous qualitie; why you shall finde,

That Heauen hath infus'd them with these Spirits,

To make them Instruments of feare, and warning,

Vnto some monstrous State.

Now could I (Caska) name to thee a man,

Most like this dreadfull Night,

That Thunders, Lightens, opens Graues, and roares,

As doth the Lyon in the Capitoll:

A man no mightier then thy selfe, or me,

In personall action; yet prodigious growne,

And fearefull, as these strange eruptions are

Cask: 'Tis Caesar that you meane:

Is it not, Cassius?

Cassi: Let it be who it is: for Romans now

Haue Thewes, and Limbes, like to their Ancestors;

But woe the while, our Fathers mindes are dead,

And we are gouern'd with our Mothers spirits,

Our yoake, and sufferance, shew vs Womanish

Cask: Indeed, they say, the Senators to morrow

Meane to establish Caesar as a King:

And he shall weare his Crowne by Sea, and Land,

In euery place, saue here in Italy

Cassi: I know where I will weare this Dagger then;

Cassius from Bondage will deliuer Cassius:

Therein, yee Gods, you make the weake most strong;

Therein, yee Gods, you Tyrants doe defeat.

Nor Stonie Tower, nor Walls of beaten Brasse,

Nor ayre-lesse Dungeon, nor strong Linkes of Iron,

Can be retentiue to the strength of spirit:

But Life being wearie of these worldly Barres,

Neuer lacks power to dismisse it selfe.

If I know this, know all the World besides,

That part of Tyrannie that I doe beare,

I can shake off at pleasure.

Thunder still.

Cask: So can I:

So euery Bond-man in his owne hand beares

The power to cancell his Captiuitie

Cassi: And why should César be a Tyrant then?

Poore man, I know he would not be a Wolfe,

But that he sees the Romans are but Sheepe:

He were no Lyon, were not Romans Hindes.

Those that with haste will make a mightie fire,

Begin it with weake Strawes. What trash is Rome?

What Rubbish, and what Offall? when it serues

For the base matter, to illuminate

So vile a thing as Caesar. But oh Griefe,

Where hast thou led me? I (perhaps) speake this

Before a willing Bond-man: then I know

My answere must be made. But I am arm'd,

And dangers are to me indifferent

Cask: You speake to Caska, and to such a man,

That is no flearing Tell-tale. Hold, my Hand:

Be factious for redresse of all these Griefes,

And I will set this foot of mine as farre,

As who goes farthest

Cassi: There's a Bargaine made.

Now know you, Caska, I haue mou'd already

Some certaine of the Noblest minded Romans

To vnder-goe, with me, an Enterprize,

Of Honorable dangerous consequence;

And I doe know by this, they stay for me

In Pompeyes Porch: for now this fearefull Night,

There is no stirre, or walking in the streetes;

And the Complexion of the Element

Is Fauors, like the Worke we haue in hand,

Most bloodie, fierie, and most terrible.

Enter Cinna.

Caska: Stand close a while, for heere comes one in haste

Cassi: 'Tis Cinna, I doe know him by his Gate,

He is a friend. Cinna, where haste you so?

Cinna: To finde out you: Who's that, Metellus Cymber?

Cassi: No, it is Caska, one incorporate

To our Attempts. Am I not stay'd for, Cinna?

Cinna: I am glad on't.

What a fearefull Night is this?

There's two or three of vs haue seene strange sights

Cassi: Am I not stay'd for? tell me

Cinna: Yes, you are. O Cassius,

If you could but winne the Noble Brutus

To our party-

Cassi: Be you content. Good Cinna, take this Paper,

And looke you lay it in the Pretors Chayre,

Where Brutus may but finde it: and throw this

In at his Window; set this vp with Waxe

Vpon old Brutus Statue: all this done,

Repaire to Pompeyes Porch, where you shall finde vs.

Is Decius Brutus and Trebonius there?

Cinna: All, but Metellus Cymber, and hee's gone

To seeke you at your house. Well, I will hie,

And so bestow these Papers as you bad me

Cassi: That done, repayre to Pompeyes Theater.

Exit Cinna.

Come Caska, you and I will yet, ere day,

See Brutus at his house: three parts of him

Is ours alreadie, and the man entire

Vpon the next encounter, yeelds him ours

Cask: O, he sits high in all the Peoples hearts:

And that which would appeare Offence in vs,

His Countenance, like richest Alchymie,

Will change to Vertue, and to Worthinesse

Cassi: Him, and his worth, and our great need of him,

You haue right well conceited: let vs goe,

For it is after Mid-night, and ere day,

We will awake him, and be sure of him.

Exeunt.

Actus Secundus

Enter Brutus in his Orchard.

Brut: What Lucius, hoe?
           I cannot, by the progresse of the Starres,
           Giue guesse how neere to day- Lucius, I say?
           I would it were my fault to sleepe so soundly.
           When Lucius, when? awake, I say: what Lucius?

Enter Lucius.

Luc: Call'd you, my Lord?

Brut: Get me a Tapor in my Study, Lucius:
           When it is lighted, come and call me here

Luc: I will, my Lord.

Enter.

Brut: It must be by his death: and for my part,
           I know no personall cause, to spurne at him,
           But for the generall. He would be crown'd:
           How that might change his nature, there's the question?
           It is the bright day, that brings forth the Adder,

And that craues warie walking: Crowne him that,

And then I graunt we put a Sting in him,

That at his will he may doe danger with.

Th' abuse of Greatnesse, is, when it dis-ioynes

Remorse from Power: And to speake truth of Caesar,

I haue not knowne, when his Affections sway'd

More then his Reason. But 'tis a common proofe,

That Lowlynesse is young Ambitions Ladder,

Whereto the Climber vpward turnes his Face:

But when he once attaines the vpmost Round,

He then vnto the Ladder turnes his Backe,

Lookes in the Clouds, scorning the base degrees

By which he did ascend: so Caesar may;

Then least he may, preuent. And since the Quarrell

Will beare no colour, for the thing he is,

Fashion it thus; that what he is, augmented,

Would runne to these, and these extremities:

And therefore thinke him as a Serpents egge,

Which hatch'd, would as his kinde grow mis-chieuous;

And kill him in the shell.

Enter Lucius.

Luc: The Taper burneth in your Closet, Sir:

Searching the Window for a Flint, I found

This Paper, thus seal'd vp, and I am sure

It did not lye there when I went to Bed.

Giues him the Letter.

Brut: Get you to Bed againe, it is not day:

Is not to morrow (Boy) the first of March?

Luc: I know not, Sir

Brut: Looke in the Calender, and bring me word

Luc: I will, Sir.

Enter.

Brut: The exhalations, whizzing in the ayre,

Giue so much light, that I may reade by them.

Opens the Letter, and reades.

Brutus thou sleep'st; awake, and see thy selfe:

Shall Rome, &c. speake, strike, redresse.

Brutus, thou sleep'st: awake.

Such instigations haue beene often dropt,

Where I haue tooke them vp:

Shall Rome, &c. Thus must I piece it out:

Shall Rome stand vnder one mans awe? What Rome?

My Ancestors did from the streetes of Rome

The Tarquin driue, when he was call'd a King.

Speake, strike, redresse. Am I entreated

To speake, and strike? O Rome, I make thee promise,

If the redresse will follow, thou receiuest

Thy full Petition at the hand of Brutus.

Enter Lucius.

Luc: Sir, March is wasted fifteene dayes.

  Knocke within.

Brut: 'Tis good. Go to the Gate, some body knocks:

  Since Cassius first did whet me against Caesar,

  I haue not slept.

  Betweene the acting of a dreadfull thing,

  And the first motion, all the Interim is

  Like a Phantasma, or a hideous Dreame:

  The Genius, and the mortall Instruments

  Are then in councell; and the state of a man,

  Like to a little Kingdome, suffers then

  The nature of an Insurrection.

Enter Lucius.

Luc: Sir, 'tis your Brother Cassius at the Doore,

  Who doth desire to see you

Brut: Is he alone?

Luc: No, Sir, there are moe with him

Brut: Doe you know them?

Luc: No, Sir, their Hats are pluckt about their Eares,

          And halfe their Faces buried in their Cloakes,

          That by no meanes I may discouer them,

          By any marke of fauour

Brut: Let 'em enter:

          They are the Faction. O Conspiracie,

          Sham'st thou to shew thy dang'rous Brow by Night,

          When euills are most free? O then, by day

          Where wilt thou finde a Cauerne darke enough,

          To maske thy monstrous Visage? Seek none Conspiracie,

          Hide it in Smiles, and Affabilitie:

          For if thou path thy natiue semblance on,

          Not Erebus it selfe were dimme enough,

          To hide thee from preuention.

Enter the Conspirators, Cassius, Caska, Decius, Cinna, Metellus, and Trebonius.

Cass: I thinke we are too bold vpon your Rest:

          Good morrow Brutus, doe we trouble you?

Brut: I haue beene vp this howre, awake all Night:

          Know I these men, that come along with you?

Cass: Yes, euery man of them; and no man here

          But honors you: and euery one doth wish,

You had but that opinion of your selfe,

Which euery Noble Roman beares of you.

This is Trebonius

Brut: He is welcome hither

Cass: This, Decius Brutus

Brut: He is welcome too

Cass: This, Caska; this, Cinna; and this, Metellus Cymber

Brut: They are all welcome.

What watchfull Cares doe interpose themselues

Betwixt your Eyes, and Night?

Cass: Shall I entreat a word?

They whisper.

Decius: Here lyes the East: doth not the Day breake heere?

Cask: No

Cin: O pardon, Sir, it doth; and yon grey Lines, That fret the Clouds, are Messengers of Day

Cask: You shall confesse, that you are both deceiu›d:

Heere, as I point my Sword, the Sunne arises,

Which is a great way growing on the South,

Weighing the youthfull Season of the yeare.

Some two moneths hence, vp higher toward the North

He first presents his fire, and the high East

    Stands as the Capitoll, directly heere

Bru: Giue me your hands all ouer, one by one

Cas: And let vs sweare our Resolution

Brut: No, not an Oath: if not the Face of men,

    The sufferance of our Soules, the times Abuse;

    If these be Motiues weake, breake off betimes,

    And euery man hence, to his idle bed:

    So let high-sighted-Tyranny range on,

    Till each man drop by Lottery. But if these

    (As I am sure they do) beare fire enough

    To kindle Cowards, and to steele with valour

    The melting Spirits of women. Then Country-
men,

    What neede we any spurre, but our owne cause

    To pricke vs to redresse? What other Bond,

    Then secret Romans, that haue spoke the word,

    And will not palter? And what other Oath,

    Then Honesty to Honesty ingag'd,

    That this shall be, or we will fall for it.

    Sweare Priests and Cowards, and men Caute-
lous

    Old feeble Carrions, and such suffering Soules

    That welcome wrongs: Vnto bad causes, sweare

    Such Creatures as men doubt; but do not staine

    The euen vertue of our Enterprize,

Nor th' insuppressiue Mettle of our Spirits,

To thinke, that or our Cause, or our Performance

mance

Did neede an Oath. When euery drop of blood

That euery Roman beares, and Nobly beares

Is guilty of a seuerall Bastardie,

If he do breake the smallest Particle

Of any promise that hath past from him

Cas: But what of Cicero? Shall we sound him?

I thinke he will stand very strong with vs

Cask: Let vs not leaue him out

Cyn: No, by no meanes

Metel: O let vs haue him, for his Siluer haires

Will purchase vs a good opinion:

And buy mens voyces, to commend our deeds:

It shall be sayd, his iudgement rul'd our hands,

Our youths, and wildenesse, shall no whit appeare,

peare,

Bru: O name him not; let vs not breake with him,

For he will neuer follow any thing

That other men begin

Cas: Then leaue him out

Cask: Indeed, he is not fit

Decius: Shall no man else be toucht, but onely Caesar?

Cas: Decius well vrg'd: I thinke it is not meet,

Marke Antony, so well belou'd of Caesar,

Should out-liue Caesar, we shall finde of him

A shrew'd Contriuer. And you know, his meanes

If he improue them, may well stretch so farre

As to annoy vs all: which to preuent,

Let Antony and Caesar fall together

Bru:　Our course will seeme too bloody, Caius Cassius,

To cut the Head off, and then hacke the Limbes:

Like Wrath in death, and Enuy afterwards:

For Antony, is but a Limbe of Caesar.

Let's be Sacrificers, but not Butchers Caius:

We all stand vp against the spirit of Caesar,

And in the Spirit of men, there is no blood:

O that we then could come by Caesars Spirit,

And not dismember Caesar! But (alas)

Caesar must bleed for it. And gentle Friends,

Let's kill him Boldly, but not Wrathfully:

Let's carue him, as a Dish fit for the Gods,

Not hew him as a Carkasse fit for Hounds:

And let our Hearts, as subtle Masters do,

Stirre vp their Seruants to an acte of Rage,

And after seeme to chide 'em. This shall make

Our purpose Necessary, and not Enuious.

Which so appearing to the common eyes,

We shall be call'd Purgers, not Murderers.

	And for Marke Antony, thinke not of him:
	For he can do no more then Caesars Arme,
	When Caesars head is off
Cas:	Yet I feare him,
	For in the ingrafted loue he beares to Caesar
Bru:	Alas, good Cassius, do not thinke of him:
	If he loue Caesar, all that he can do
	Is to himselfe; take thought, and dye for Caesar,
	And that were much he should: for he is giuen
	To sports, to wildenesse, and much company
Treb:	There is no feare in him; let him not dye,
	For he will liue, and laugh at this heereafter.

Clocke strikes.

Bru:	Peace, count the Clocke
Cas:	The Clocke hath stricken three
Treb:	'Tis time to part
Cass:	But it is doubtfull yet,
	Whether Caesar will come forth to day, or no:
	For he is Superstitious growne of late,
	Quite from the maine Opinion he held once,
	Of Fantasie, of Dreames, and Ceremonies:
	It may be, these apparant Prodigies,
	The vnaccustom'd Terror of this night,
	And the perswasion of his Augurers,

	May hold him from the Capitoll to day
Decius:	Neuer feare that: If he be so resolu›d,
	I can ore-sway him: For he loues to heare,
	That Vnicornes may be betray'd with Trees,
	And Beares with Glasses, Elephants with Holes,
	Lyons with Toyles, and men with Flatterers.
	But, when I tell him, he hates Flatterers,
	He sayes, he does; being then most flattered.
	Let me worke:
	For I can giue his humour the true bent;
	And I will bring him to the Capitoll
Cas:	Nay, we will all of vs, be there to fetch him
Bru:	By the eight houre, is that the vttermost?
Cin:	Be that the vttermost, and faile not then
Met:	Caius Ligarius doth beare Caesar hard,
	Who rated him for speaking well of Pompey;
	I wonder none of you haue thought of him
Bru:	Now good Metellus go along by him:
	He loues me well, and I haue giuen him Reasons,
	Send him but hither, and Ile fashion him
Cas:	The morning comes vpon›s:
	Wee'l leaue you Brutus,
	And Friends disperse your selues; but all remem-
	ber
	What you haue said, and shew your selues true
	Romans

Bru: Good Gentlemen, looke fresh and merrily,

          Let not our lookes put on our purposes,

          But beare it as our Roman Actors do,

          With vntyr'd Spirits, and formall Constancie,

          And so good morrow to you euery one.

Exeunt.

Manet Brutus

Boy: Lucius: Fast asleepe? It is no matter,

Enioy the hony-heauy-Dew of Slumber:

Thou hast no Figures, nor no Fantasies,

Which busie care drawes, in the braines of men;

Therefore thou sleep'st so sound.

Enter Portia.

Por: Brutus, my Lord

Bru: Portia: What meane you? wherfore rise you now?

It is not for your health, thus to commit

Your weake condition, to the raw cold morning

Por: Nor for yours neither. Y›haue vngently Brutus

Stole from my bed: and yesternight at Supper

You sodainly arose, and walk'd about,

Musing, and sighing, with your armes acrosse

And when I ask'd you what the matter was,

You star'd vpon me, with vngentle lookes.

I vrg'd you further, then you scratch'd your head,

And too impatiently stampt with your foote:

Yet I insisted, yet you answer'd not,

But with an angry wafter of your hand

Gaue signe for me to leaue you: So I did,

Fearing to strengthen that impatience

Which seem'd too much inkindled; and withall,

Hoping it was but an effect of Humor,

Which sometime hath his houre with euery man.

It will not let you eate, nor talke, nor sleepe;

And could it worke so much vpon your shape,

As it hath much preuayl'd on your Condition,

I should not know you Brutus. Deare my Lord,

Make me acquainted with your cause of greefe

Bru:	I am not well in health, and that is all
Por:	Brutus is wise, and were he not in health,
	He would embrace the meanes to come by it
Bru:	Why so I do: good Portia go to bed
Por:	Is Brutus sicke? And is it Physicall

To walke vnbraced, and sucke vp the humours

Of the danke Morning? What, is Brutus sicke?

And will he steale out of his wholsome bed

To dare the vile contagion of the Night?

And tempt the Rhewmy, and vnpurged Ayre,

To adde vnto his sicknesse? No my Brutus,

You haue some sicke Offence within your minde,

Which by the Right and Vertue of my place

I ought to know of: And vpon my knees,

I charme you, by my once commended Beauty,

By all your vowes of Loue, and that great Vow

Which did incorporate and make vs one,

That you vnfold to me, your selfe; your halfe

Why you are heauy: and what men to night

Haue had resort to you: for heere haue beene

Some sixe or seuen, who did hide their faces

Euen from darknesse

Bru: Kneele not gentle Portia

Por: I should not neede, if you were gentle Brutus.

Within the Bond of Marriage, tell me Brutus,

Is it excepted, I should know no Secrets

That appertaine to you? Am I your Selfe,

But as it were in sort, or limitation?

To keepe with you at Meales, comfort your Bed,

And talke to you sometimes? Dwell I but in the Suburbs

Of your good pleasure? If it be no more,

Portia is Brutus Harlot, not his Wife

Bru: You are my true and honourable Wife,

As deere to me, as are the ruddy droppes

That visit my sad heart

Por: If this were true, then should I know this secret.

I graunt I am a Woman; but withall,

A Woman that Lord Brutus tooke to Wife:

I graunt I am a Woman; but withall,

A Woman well reputed: Cato's Daughter.

Thinke you, I am no stronger then my Sex

Being so Father'd, and so Husbanded?

Tell me your Counsels, I will not disclose 'em:

I haue made strong proofe of my Constancie,

Giuing my selfe a voluntary wound

Heere, in the Thigh: Can I beare that with patience,

And not my Husbands Secrets?

Bru: O ye Gods!

Render me worthy of this Noble Wife.

Knocke.

Harke, harke, one knockes: Portia go in a while,

And by and by thy bosome shall partake

The secrets of my Heart.

All my engagements, I will construe to thee,

All the Charractery of my sad browes:

Leaue me with hast.

Exit Portia.

Enter Lucius and Ligarius.

Lucius, who's that knockes

Luc: Heere is a sicke man that would speak with you

Bru:	Caius Ligarius, that Metellus spake of.
	Boy, stand aside. Caius Ligarius, how?
Cai:	Vouchsafe good morrow from a feeble tongue
Bru:	O what a time haue you chose out braue Caius
	To weare a Kerchiefe? Would you were not sicke
Cai:	I am not sicke, if Brutus haue in hand
	Any exploit worthy the name of Honor
Bru:	Such an exploit haue I in hand Ligarius,
	Had you a healthfull eare to heare of it
Cai:	By all the Gods that Romans bow before,
	I heere discard my sicknesse. Soule of Rome,
	Braue Sonne, deriu'd from Honourable Loines,
	Thou like an Exorcist, hast coniur'd vp
	My mortified Spirit. Now bid me runne,
	And I will striue with things impossible,
	Yea get the better of them. What's to do?
Bru:	A peece of worke,
	That will make sicke men whole
Cai:	But are not some whole, that we must make sicke?
Bru:	That must we also. What it is my Caius,
	I shall vnfold to thee, as we are going,
	To whom it must be done
Cai:	Set on your foote,
	And with a heart new-fir'd, I follow you,

> To do I know not what: but it sufficeth
> That Brutus leads me on.

Thunder

Bru: Follow me then.

Exeunt.

Thunder & Lightning

Enter Iulius Caesar in his Night-gowne.

Caesar: Nor Heauen, nor Earth,
>   Haue beene at peace to night:
>   Thrice hath Calphurnia, in her sleepe cryed out,
>   Helpe, ho: They murther Caesar. Who's within?

Enter a Seruant.

Ser: My Lord

Caes Go bid the Priests do present Sacrifice,

And bring me their opinions of Successe

Ser: I will my Lord.

Exit

Enter Calphurnia.

Cal: What mean you Caesar? Thin you to walk forth?
>   You shall not stirre out of your house to day
>   Caes Caesar shall forth; the things that threaten'd
>   me,

Ne're look'd but on my backe: When they shall see

The face of Caesar, they are vanished

Calp: Caesar, I neuer stood on Ceremonies,

Yet now they fright me: There is one within,

Besides the things that we haue heard and seene,

Recounts most horrid sights seene by the Watch.

A Lionnesse hath whelped in the streets,

And Graues haue yawn'd, and yeelded vp their dead;

Fierce fiery Warriours fight vpon the Clouds

In Rankes and Squadrons, and right forme of Warre

Which drizel'd blood vpon the Capitoll:

The noise of Battell hurtled in the Ayre:

Horsses do neigh, and dying men did grone,

And Ghosts did shrieke and squeale about the streets.

O Caesar, these things are beyond all vse,

And I do feare them

Caes What can be auoyded

Whose end is purpos'd by the mighty Gods?

Yet Caesar shall go forth: for these Predictions

Are to the world in generall, as to Caesar

Calp: When Beggers dye, there are no Comets seen,

The Heauens themselues blaze forth the death of Princes

   Caes Cowards dye many times before their deaths,

   The valiant neuer taste of death but once:

   Of all the Wonders that I yet haue heard,

   It seemes to me most strange that men should feare,

   Seeing that death, a necessary end

   Will come, when it will come.

Enter a Seruant.

What say the Augurers?

Ser: They would not haue you to stirre forth to day.

   Plucking the intrailes of an Offering forth,

   They could not finde a heart within the beast

   Caes The Gods do this in shame of Cowardice:

   Caesar should be a Beast without a heart

   If he should stay at home to day for feare:

   No Caesar shall not; Danger knowes full well

   That Caesar is more dangerous then he.

   We heare two Lyons litter'd in one day,

   And I the elder and more terrible,

   And Caesar shall go foorth

Calp: Alas my Lord,

   Your wisedome is consum'd in confidence:

   Do not go forth to day: Call it my feare,

That keepes you in the house, and not your
owne.

Wee'l send Mark Antony to the Senate house,

And he shall say, you are not well to day:

Let me vpon my knee, preuaile in this

Caes Mark Antony shall say I am not well,

And for thy humor, I will stay at home.

Enter Decius.

Heere's Decius Brutus, he shall tell them so

Deci: Caesar, all haile: Good morrow worthy Caesar,

          I come to fetch you to the Senate house

          Caes And you are come in very happy time,

          To beare my greeting to the Senators,

          And tell them that I will not come to day:

          Cannot, is false: and that I dare not, falser:

          I will not come to day, tell them so Decius

Calp: Say he is sicke

          Caes Shall Caesar send a Lye?

          Haue I in Conquest stretcht mine Arme so farre,

          To be afear'd to tell Gray-beards the truth:

          Decius, go tell them, Caesar will not come

Deci: Most mighty Caesar, let me know some cause,

          Lest I be laught at when I tell them so

          Caes The cause is in my Will, I will not come,

          That is enough to satisfie the Senate.

But for your priuate satisfaction,

Because I loue you, I will let you know.

Calphurnia heere my wife, stayes me at home:

She dreampt to night, she saw my Statue,

Which like a Fountaine, with an hundred spouts

Did run pure blood: and many lusty Romans

Came smiling, & did bathe their hands in it:

And these does she apply, for warnings and por-
tents,

And euils imminent; and on her knee

Hath begg'd, that I will stay at home to day

Deci: This Dreame is all amisse interpreted,

It was a vision, faire and fortunate:

Your Statue spouting blood in many pipes,

In which so many smiling Romans bath'd,

Signifies, that from you great Rome shall sucke

Reuiuing blood, and that great men shall presse

For Tinctures, Staines, Reliques, and Cogni-
sance.

This by Calphurnia's Dreame is signified

Caes And this way haue you well expounded it

Deci: I haue, when you haue heard what I can say:

And know it now, the Senate haue concluded

To giue this day, a Crowne to mighty Caesar.

If you shall send them word you will not come,

Their mindes may change. Besides, it were a mocke

Apt to be render'd, for some one to say,

Breake vp the Senate, till another time:

When Caesars wife shall meete with better Dreames

If Caesar hide himselfe, shall they not whisper

Loe Caesar is affraid?

Pardon me Caesar, for my deere deere loue

To your proceeding, bids me tell you this:

And reason to my loue is liable

Caes How foolish do your fears seeme now Calphurnia?

I am ashamed I did yeeld to them.

Giue me my Robe, for I will go.

Enter Brutus, Ligarius, Metellus, Caska, Trebonius, Cynna, and Publius.

And looke where Publius is come to fetch me

Pub: Good morrow Caesar

Caes Welcome Publius.

What Brutus, are you stirr'd so earely too?

Good morrow Caska: Caius Ligarius,

Caesar was ne're so much your enemy,

As that same Ague which hath made you leane.

What is't a Clocke?

Bru: Caesar, 'tis strucken eight

        Caes I thanke you for your paines and curtesie.

Enter Antony.

See, Antony that Reuels long a-nights

Is notwithstanding vp. Good morrow Antony

Ant: So to most Noble Caesar

        Caes Bid them prepare within:

        I am too blame to be thus waited for.

        Now Cynna, now Metellus: what Trebonius,

        I haue an houres talke in store for you:

        Remember that you call on me to day:

        Be neere me, that I may remember you

Treb: Caesar I will: and so neere will I be,

        That your best Friends shall wish I had beene
        further

        Caes Good Friends go in, and taste some wine
        with me.

        And we (like Friends) will straight way go to-
        gether

Bru: That euery like is not the same, O Caesar,

The heart of Brutus earnes to thinke vpon.

Exeunt.

Enter Artemidorus.

Caesar, beware of Brutus, take heede of Cassius; come not
neere Caska, haue an eye to Cynna, trust not Trebonius,

marke well Metellus Cymber, Decius Brutus loues thee
not: Thou hast wrong'd Caius Ligarius. There is but one
minde in all these men, and it is bent against Caesar: If
thou beest not Immortall, looke about you: Security giues way to Conspiracie. The mighty Gods defend thee.
Thy Louer, Artemidorus. Heere will I stand, till Caesar
passe along, And as a Sutor will I giue him this: My heart
laments, that Vertue cannot liue Out of the teeth of Em-
ulation. If thou reade this, O Caesar, thou mayest liue; If
not, the Fates with Traitors do contriue.

Enter.

Enter Portia and Lucius.

Por:	I prythee Boy, run to the Senate-house,
	Stay not to answer me, but get thee gone.
	Why doest thou stay?
Luc:	To know my errand Madam
Por:	I would haue had thee there and heere agen
	Ere I can tell thee what thou should'st do there:
	O Constancie, be strong vpon my side,
	Set a huge Mountaine 'tweene my Heart and Tongue:
	I haue a mans minde, but a womans might:
	How hard it is for women to keepe counsell.
	Art thou heere yet?
Lu:	Madam, what should I do?
	Run to the Capitoll, and nothing else?

And so returne to you, and nothing else?

Por: Yes, bring me word Boy, if thy Lord look well,

For he went sickly forth: and take good note

What Caesar doth, what Sutors presse to him.

Hearke Boy, what noyse is that?

Luc: I heare none Madam

Por: Prythee listen well:

I heard a bussling Rumor like a Fray,

And the winde brings it from the Capitoll

Luc: Sooth Madam, I heare nothing.

Enter the Soothsayer.

Por: Come hither Fellow, which way hast thou bin?

Sooth: At mine owne house, good Lady

Por: What is›t a clocke?

Sooth: About the ninth houre Lady

Por: Is Caesar yet gone to the Capitoll?

Sooth: Madam not yet, I go to take my stand,

To see him passe on to the Capitoll

Por: Thou hast some suite to Caesar, hast thou not?

Sooth: That I haue Lady, if it will please Caesar

To be so good to Caesar, as to heare me:

I shall beseech him to befriend himselfe

Por: Why know›st thou any harme›s intended towards him?

Sooth: None that I know will be,

Much that I feare may chance:

Good morrow to you: heere the street is narrow:

The throng that followes Caesar at the heeles,

Of Senators, of Praetors, common Sutors,

Will crowd a feeble man (almost) to death:

Ile get me to a place more voyd, and there

Speake to great Caesar as he comes along.

Exit

Por: I must go in:

Aye me! How weake a thing

The heart of woman is? O Brutus,

The Heauens speede thee in thine enterprize.

Sure the Boy heard me: Brutus hath a suite

That Caesar will not grant. O, I grow faint:

Run Lucius, and commend me to my Lord,

Say I am merry; Come to me againe,

And bring me word what he doth say to thee.

Exeunt.

Actus Tertius

Flourish

**Enter Caesar, Brutus, Cassius, Caska, Decius, Me-
tellus, Trebonius, Cynna, Antony, Lepidus, Artime-
dorus, Publius, and the Soothsayer.**

Caes The Ides of March are come

Sooth: I Caesar, but not gone

Art: Haile Caesar: Read this Scedule

Deci: Trebonius doth desire you to ore-read

   (At your best leysure) this his humble suite

Art: O Caesar, reade mine first: for mine›s a suite

   That touches Caesar neerer. Read it great Caesar

   Caes What touches vs our selfe, shall be last se-
ru'd

Art: Delay not Caesar, read it instantly

   Caes What, is the fellow mad?

Pub: Sirra, giue place

Cassi: What, vrge you your Petitions in the street?

   Come to the Capitoll

Popil: I wish your enterprize to day may thriue

Cassi:	What enterprize Popillius?
Popil:	Fare you well
Bru:	What said Popillius Lena?
Cassi:	He wisht to day our enterprize might thriue:
	I feare our purpose is discouered
Bru:	Looke how he makes to Caesar: marke him
Cassi:	Caska be sodaine, for we feare preuention.
	Brutus what shall be done? If this be knowne,
	Cassius or Caesar neuer shall turne backe,
	For I will slay my selfe
Bru:	Cassius be constant:
	Popillius Lena speakes not of our purposes,
	For looke he smiles, and Caesar doth not change
Cassi:	Trebonius knowes his time: for look you Brutus
	He drawes Mark Antony out of the way
Deci:	Where is Metellus Cimber, let him go,
	And presently preferre his suite to Caesar
Bru:	He is addrest: presse neere, and second him
Cin:	Caska, you are the first that reares your hand
	Caes Are we all ready? What is now amisse,
	That Caesar and his Senate must redresse?
Metel:	Most high, most mighty, and most puisant Cae-sar
	Metellus Cymber throwes before thy Seate
	An humble heart

	Caes I must preuent thee Cymber:
	These couchings, and these lowly courtesies
	Might fire the blood of ordinary men,
	And turne pre-Ordinance, and first Decree
	Into the lane of Children. Be not fond,
	To thinke that Caesar beares such Rebell blood
	That will be thaw'd from the true quality
	With that which melteth Fooles, I meane sweet words,
	Low-crooked-curtsies, and base Spaniell fawning:
	Thy Brother by decree is banished:
	If thou doest bend, and pray, and fawne for him,
	I spurne thee like a Curre out of my way:
	Know, Caesar doth not wrong, nor without cause
	Will he be satisfied
Metel:	Is there no voyce more worthy then my owne,
	To sound more sweetly in great Caesars eare,
	For the repealing of my banish'd Brother?
Bru:	I kisse thy hand, but not in flattery Caesar:
	Desiring thee, that Publius Cymber may
	Haue an immediate freedome of repeale
	Caes What Brutus?
Cassi:	Pardon Caesar: Caesar pardon:
	As lowe as to thy foote doth Cassius fall,
	To begge infranchisement for Publius Cymber

Caes I could be well mou'd, if I were as you,

If I could pray to mooue, Prayers would mooue me:

But I am constant as the Northerne Starre,

Of whose true fixt, and resting quality,

There is no fellow in the Firmament.

The Skies are painted with vnnumbred sparkes,

They are all Fire, and euery one doth shine:

But, there's but one in all doth hold his place.

So, in the World; 'Tis furnish'd well with Men,

And Men are Flesh and Blood, and apprehensiue;

Yet in the number, I do know but One

That vnassayleable holds on his Ranke,\Vnshak'd of Motion: and that I am he,

Let me a little shew it, euen in this:

That I was constant Cymber should be banish'd,

And constant do remaine to keepe him so

Cinna: O Caesar

Caes Hence: Wilt thou lift vp Olympus?

Decius: Great Caesar

Caes Doth not Brutus bootlesse kneele?

Cask: Speake hands for me.

They stab Caesar.

Caes Et Tu Brute? - Then fall Caesar.

Dyes

Cin: Liberty, Freedome; Tyranny is dead,

         Run hence, proclaime, cry it about the Streets

Cassi: Some to the common Pulpits, and cry out

         Liberty, Freedome, and Enfranchisement

Bru: People and Senators, be not affrighted:

         Fly not, stand still: Ambitions debt is paid

Cask: Go to the Pulpit Brutus

Dec: And Cassius too

Bru: Where's Publius?

Cin: Heere, quite confounded with this mutiny

Met: Stand fast together, least some Friend of Caesars
         Should chance-

Bru: Talke not of standing. Publius good cheere,

         There is no harme intended to your person,

         Nor to no Roman else: so tell them Publius

Cassi: And leaue vs Publius, least that the people

         Rushing on vs, should do your Age some mis-
         chiefe

Bru: Do so, and let no man abide this deede,

         But we the Doers.

Enter Trebonius

Cassi: Where is Antony?

Treb: Fled to his House amaz'd:

         Men, Wiues, and Children, stare, cry out, and
         run,

	As it were Doomesday
Bru:	Fates, we will know your pleasures:
	That we shall dye we know, 'tis but the time
	And drawing dayes out, that men stand vpon
Cask:	Why he that cuts off twenty yeares of life,
	Cuts off so many yeares of fearing death
Bru:	Grant that, and then is Death a Benefit:
	So are we Caesars Friends, that haue abridg'd
	His time of fearing death. Stoope Romans, stoope,
	And let vs bathe our hands in Caesars blood
	Vp to the Elbowes, and besmeare our Swords:
	Then walke we forth, euen to the Market place,
	And wauing our red Weapons o're our heads,
	Let's all cry Peace, Freedome, and Liberty
Cassi:	Stoop then, and wash. How many Ages hence
	Shall this our lofty Scene be acted ouer,
	In State vnborne, and Accents yet vnknowne?
Bru:	How many times shall Caesar bleed in sport,
	That now on Pompeyes Basis lye along,
	No worthier then the dust?
Cassi:	So oft as that shall be,
	So often shall the knot of vs be call'd,
	The Men that gaue their Country liberty
Dec:	What, shall we forth?

Cassi: I, euery man away.

Brutus shall leade, and we will grace his heeles

With the most boldest, and best hearts of Rome.

Enter a Seruant.

Bru: Soft, who comes heere? A friend of Antonies

Ser: Thus Brutus did my Master bid me kneele;

Thus did Mark Antony bid me fall downe,

And being prostrate, thus he bad me say:

Brutus is Noble, Wise, Valiant, and Honest;

Caesar was Mighty, Bold, Royall, and Louing:

Say, I loue Brutus, and I honour him;

Say, I fear'd Caesar, honour'd him, and lou'd him.

If Brutus will vouchsafe, that Antony

May safely come to him, and be resolu'd

How Caesar hath deseru'd to lye in death,

Mark Antony, shall not loue Caesar dead

So well as Brutus liuing; but will follow

The Fortunes and Affayres of Noble Brutus,

Thorough the hazards of this vntrod State,

With all true Faith. So sayes my Master Antony

Bru: Thy Master is a Wise and Valiant Romane,

I neuer thought him worse:

Tell him, so please him come vnto this place

He shall be satisfied: and by my Honor

Depart vntouch'd

Ser: Ile fetch him presently.

Exit Seruant.

Bru: I know that we shall haue him well to Friend

Cassi: I wish we may: But yet haue I a minde

That feares him much: and my misgiuing still

Falles shrewdly to the purpose.

Enter Antony.

Bru: But heere comes Antony:

Welcome Mark Antony

Ant: O mighty Caesar! Dost thou lye so lowe?

Are all thy Conquests, Glories, Triumphes, Spoiles,

Shrunke to this little Measure? Fare thee well.

I know not Gentlemen what you intend,

Who else must be let blood, who else is ranke:

If I my selfe, there is no houre so fit

As Caesars deaths houre; nor no Instrument

Of halfe that worth, as those your Swords; made rich

With the most Noble blood of all this World.

I do beseech yee, if you beare me hard,

Now, whil'st your purpled hands do reeke and smoake,

Fulfill your pleasure. Liue a thousand yeeres,

I shall not finde my selfe so apt to dye.

No place will please me so, no meane of death,

As heere by Caesar, and by you cut off,

The Choice and Master Spirits of this Age

Bru: O Antony! Begge not your death of vs:

Though now we must appeare bloody and cruell,

As by our hands, and this our present Acte

You see we do: Yet see you but our hands,

And this, the bleeding businesse they haue done:

Our hearts you see not, they are pittifull:

And pitty to the generall wrong of Rome,

As fire driues out fire, so pitty, pitty

Hath done this deed on Caesar. For your part,

To you, our Swords haue leaden points Marke
Antony:

Our Armes in strength of malice, and our Hearts

Of Brothers temper, do receiue you in,

With all kinde loue, good thoughts, and reuerence

Cassi: Your voyce shall be as strong as any mans,

In the disposing of new Dignities

Bru: Onely be patient, till we haue appeas›d

The Multitude, beside themselues with feare,

And then, we will deliuer you the cause,

Why I, that did loue Caesar when I strooke him,

Haue thus proceeded

Ant: I doubt not of your Wisedome:

Let each man render me his bloody hand.

First Marcus Brutus will I shake with you;

Next Caius Cassius do I take your hand;

Now Decius Brutus yours; now yours Metellus;

Yours Cinna; and my valiant Caska, yours;

Though last, not least in loue, yours good Trebonius.

Gentlemen all: Alas, what shall I say,

My credit now stands on such slippery ground,

That one of two bad wayes you must conceit me,

Either a Coward, or a Flatterer.

That I did loue thee Caesar, O 'tis true:

If then thy Spirit looke vpon vs now,

Shall it not greeue thee deerer then thy death,

To see thy Antony making his peace,

Shaking the bloody fingers of thy Foes?

Most Noble, in the presence of thy Coarse,

Had I as many eyes, as thou hast wounds,

Weeping as fast as they streame forth thy blood,

It would become me better, then to close

In tearmes of Friendship with thine enemies.

Pardon me Iulius, heere was't thou bay'd braue
Hart,

Heere did'st thou fall, and heere thy Hunters stand

Sign'd in thy Spoyle, and Crimson'd in thy Lethee.

O World! thou wast the Forrest to this Hart,

And this indeed, O World, the Hart of thee.

How like a Deere, stroken by many Princes,

Dost thou heere lye?

Cassi: Mark Antony

Ant: Pardon me Caius Cassius:

The Enemies of Caesar, shall say this:

Then, in a Friend, it is cold Modestie

Cassi: I blame you not for praising Caesar so.

But what compact meane you to haue with vs?

Will you be prick'd in number of our Friends,

Or shall we on, and not depend on you?

Ant: Therefore I tooke your hands, but was indeed

Sway'd from the point, by looking downe on Caesar.

Friends am I with you all, and loue you all,

Vpon this hope, that you shall giue me Reasons,

Why, and wherein, Caesar was dangerous

Bru: Or else were this a sauage Spectacle:

Our Reasons are so full of good regard,

That were you Antony, the Sonne of Caesar,

You should be satisfied

Ant: That's all I seeke,

        And am moreouer sutor, that I may

        Produce his body to the Market-place,

        And in the Pulpit as becomes a Friend,

        Speake in the Order of his Funerall

Bru: You shall Marke Antony

Cassi: Brutus, a word with you:

        You know not what you do; Do not consent

        That Antony speake in his Funerall:

        Know you how much the people may be mou'd

        By that which he will vtter

Bru: By your pardon:

        I will my selfe into the Pulpit first,

        And shew the reason of our Caesars death.

        What Antony shall speake, I will protest

        He speakes by leaue, and by permission:

        And that we are contented Caesar shall

        Haue all true Rites, and lawfull Ceremonies,

        It shall aduantage more, then do vs wrong

Cassi: I know not what may fall, I like it not

Bru: Mark Antony, heere take you Caesars body:

        You shall not in your Funerall speech blame vs,

        But speake all good you can deuise of Caesar,

        And say you doo't by our permission:

        Else shall you not haue any hand at all

About his Funerall. And you shall speake

In the same Pulpit whereto I am going,

After my speech is ended

Ant: Be it so:

I do desire no more

Bru: Prepare the body then, and follow vs.

Exeunt.

Manet Antony

O pardon me, thou bleeding peece of Earth:

That I am meeke and gentle with these Butchers.

Thou art the Ruines of the Noblest man

That euer liued in the Tide of Times.

Woe to the hand that shed this costly Blood.

Ouer thy wounds, now do I Prophesie,

(Which like dumbe mouthes do ope their Ruby lips,

To begge the voyce and vtterance of my Tongue)

A Curse shall light vpon the limbes of men;

Domesticke Fury, and fierce Ciuill strife,

Shall cumber all the parts of Italy:

Blood and destruction shall be so in vse,

And dreadfull Obiects so familiar,

That Mothers shall but smile, when they behold

Their Infants quartered with the hands of Warre:

All pitty choak'd with custome of fell deeds,

And Caesars Spirit ranging for Reuenge,

With Ate by his side, come hot from Hell,

Shall in these Confines, with a Monarkes voyce,

Cry hauocke, and let slip the Dogges of Warre,

That this foule deede, shall smell aboue the earth

With Carrion men, groaning for Buriall.

Enter Octauio's Seruant.

You serue Octauius Caesar, do you not?

Ser: I do Marke Antony

Ant: Caesar did write for him to come to Rome

Ser: He did receiue his Letters, and is comming,

          And bid me say to you by word of mouth-

          O Caesar!

Ant: Thy heart is bigge: get thee a-part and weepe:

          Passion I see is catching from mine eyes,

          Seeing those Beads of sorrow stand in thine,

          Began to water. Is thy Master comming?

Ser: He lies to night within seuen Leagues of Rome

Ant: Post backe with speede,

          And tell him what hath chanc'd:

          Heere is a mourning Rome, a dangerous Rome,

          No Rome of safety for Octauius yet,

          Hie hence, and tell him so. Yet stay a-while,

          Thou shalt not backe, till I haue borne this course

          Into the Market place: There shall I try

          In my Oration, how the People take

          The cruell issue of these bloody men,

According to the which, thou shalt discourse

To yong Octauius, of the state of things.

Lend me your hand.

Exeunt.

Enter Brutus and goes into the Pulpit, and Cassius, with the Plebeians.

Ple: We will be satisfied: let vs be satisfied

Bru: Then follow me, and giue me Audience friends.

Cassius go you into the other streete,

And part the Numbers:

Those that will heare me speake, let 'em stay heere;

Those that will follow Cassius, go with him,

And publike Reasons shall be rendred

Of Caesars death

1. Ple. I will heare Brutus speake

2. I will heare Cassius, and compare their Reasons, When seuerally we heare them rendred

3. The Noble Brutus is ascended: Silence

Bru: Be patient till the last. Romans, Countrey-men, and Louers, heare mee for my cause, and be silent, that you may heare. Beleeue me for mine Honor, and haue respect to mine Honor, that you may beleeue. Censure me in your Wisedom, and awake your Senses, that you may the better Iudge. If there bee any in this Assembly, any deere Friend of Caesars, to him I say, that Brutus loue to Caesar, was no lesse then his. If then, that Friend demand, why Brutus rose against Caesar, this is my answer: Not that I lou'd Caesar lesse, but that I lou'd Rome more. Had you rather Caesar were liuing, and dye all Slaues; then that Caesar were dead, to liue all Freemen? As Caesar lou'd mee, I weepe for him; as he was Fortunate, I reioyce at it; as he was Valiant, I honour him: But, as he was Ambitious, I slew him. There is Teares, for his Loue: Ioy, for his Fortune: Honor, for his Valour: and Death, for his Ambition. Who is heere so base, that would be a Bondman? If any, speak, for him haue I offended. Who is heere so rude, that would not be a Roman? If any, speak, for him haue I offended. Who is heere so vile, that will not loue his Countrey? If any, speake, for him haue I offended. I pause for a Reply

All: None Brutus, none

Brutus: Then none haue I offended. I haue done no more to Caesar, then you shall do to Brutus. The Question of his death, is inroll'd in the Capitoll: his Glory not extenuated, wherein he was worthy; nor his offences enforc'd, for which he suffered death. Enter Mark Antony, with Caesars body.

   Heere comes his Body, mourn'd by Marke Antony, who though he had no hand in his death, shall receiue the benefit of his dying, a place in the Co[m]monwealth, as which of you shall not. With this I depart, that as I slewe my best Louer

for the good of Rome, I haue the same Dagger
for my selfe, when it shall please my Country to
need my death

All: Liue Brutus, liue, liue

1. Bring him with Triumph home vnto his house

2. Giue him a Statue with his Ancestors

3. Let him be Caesar

4. Caesars better parts, Shall be Crown'd in Brutus

1. Wee'l bring him to his House,

   With Showts and Clamors

Bru: My Country-men

2. Peace, silence, Brutus speakes

1. Peace ho

Bru: Good Countrymen, let me depart alone,

   And (for my sake) stay heere with Antony:

   Do grace to Caesars Corpes, and grace his
   Speech

   Tending to Caesars Glories, which Marke Antony

   (By our permission) is allow'd to make.

   I do intreat you, not a man depart,

   Saue I alone, till Antony haue spoke.

Exit

1 Stay ho, and let vs heare Mark Antony

3 Let him go vp into the publike Chaire, Wee'l heare him:
   Noble Antony go vp

Ant: For Brutus sake, I am beholding to you

4 What does he say of Brutus?

3 He sayes, for Brutus sake

He findes himselfe beholding to vs all

4 'Twere best he speake no harme of Brutus heere?

1 This Caesar was a Tyrant

3 Nay that's certaine:

We are blest that Rome is rid of him

2 Peace, let vs heare what Antony can say

Ant: You gentle Romans

All: Peace hoe, let vs heare him

An: Friends, Romans, Countrymen, lend me your
         ears:

         I come to bury Caesar, not to praise him:

         The euill that men do, liues after them,

         The good is oft enterred with their bones,

         So let it be with Caesar. The Noble Brutus,

         Hath told you Caesar was Ambitious:

         If it were so, it was a greeuous Fault,

         And greeuously hath Caesar answer'd it.

         Heere, vnder leaue of Brutus, and the rest

         (For Brutus is an Honourable man,

         So are they all; all Honourable men)

Come I to speake in Caesars Funerall.

He was my Friend, faithfull, and iust to me;

But Brutus sayes, he was Ambitious,

And Brutus is an Honourable man.

He hath brought many Captiues home to Rome,

Whose Ransomes, did the generall Coffers fill:

Did this in Caesar seeme Ambitious?

When that the poore haue cry'de, Caesar hath wept:

Ambition should be made of sterner stuffe,

Yet Brutus sayes, he was Ambitious:

And Brutus is an Honourable man.

You all did see, that on the Lupercall,

I thrice presented him a Kingly Crowne,

Which he did thrice refuse. Was this Ambition?

Yet Brutus sayes, he was Ambitious:

And sure he is an Honourable man.

I speake not to disprooue what Brutus spoke,

But heere I am, to speake what I do know;

You all did loue him once, not without cause,

What cause with-holds you then, to mourne for him?

O Iudgement! thou are fled to brutish Beasts,

And Men haue lost their Reason. Beare with me,

My heart is in the Coffin there with Caesar,

And I must pawse, till it come backe to me

1 Me thinkes there is much reason in his sayings

2 If thou consider rightly of the matter, Caesar ha's had great wrong

3 Ha's hee Masters? I feare there will a worse come in his place

4 Mark'd ye his words? he would not take y Crown, Therefore 'tis certaine, he was not Ambitious

1. If it be found so, some will deere abide it

2. Poore soule, his eyes are red as fire with weeping

3. There's not a Nobler man in Rome then Antony

4. Now marke him, he begins againe to speake

Ant: But yesterday, the word of Caesar might

Haue stood against the World: Now lies he there,

And none so poore to do him reuerence.

O Maisters! If I were dispos'd to stirre

Your hearts and mindes to Mutiny and Rage,

I should do Brutus wrong, and Cassius wrong:

Who (you all know) are Honourable men.

I will not do them wrong: I rather choose

To wrong the dead, to wrong my selfe and you,

Then I will wrong such Honourable men.

But heere's a Parchment, with the Seale of Caesar,

I found it in his Closset, 'tis his Will:

Let but the Commons heare this Testament:

(Which pardon me) I do not meane to reade,

And they would go and kisse dead Caesars wounds,

And dip their Napkins in his Sacred Blood;

Yea, begge a haire of him for Memory,

And dying, mention it within their Willes,

Bequeathing it as a rich Legacie

Vnto their issue

4　Wee'l heare the Will, reade it Marke Antony

All:　　The Will, the Will; we will heare Caesars Will

Ant:　　Haue patience gentle Friends, I must not read it.

It is not meete you know how Caesar lou'd you:

You are not Wood, you are not Stones, but men:

And being men, hearing the Will of Caesar,

It will inflame you, it will make you mad:

'Tis good you know not that you are his Heires,

For if you should, O what would come of it?

4　Read the Will, wee'l heare it Antony:

You shall reade vs the Will, Caesars Will

Ant:　　Will you be Patient? Will you stay a-while?

I haue o're-shot my selfe to tell you of it,

I feare I wrong the Honourable men,

Whose Daggers haue stabb'd Caesar: I do feare it

4　They were Traitors: Honourable men?

All: The Will, the Testament

2 They were Villaines, Murderers: the Will, read the Will

Ant: You will compell me then to read the Will:

          Then make a Ring about the Corpes of Caesar,

          And let me shew you him that made the Will:

          Shall I descend? And will you giue me leaue?

All: Come downe

2 Descend

3 You shall haue leaue

4 A Ring, stand round

1 Stand from the Hearse, stand from the Body

2 Roome for Antony, most Noble Antony

Ant: Nay presse not so vpon me, stand farre off

All: Stand backe: roome, beare backe

Ant: If you haue teares, prepare to shed them now.

          You all do know this Mantle, I remember

          The first time euer Caesar put it on,

          'Twas on a Summers Euening in his Tent,

          That day he ouercame the Neruij.

          Looke, in this place ran Cassius Dagger through:

          See what a rent the enuious Caska made:

          Through this, the wel-beloued Brutus stabb'd,

          And as he pluck'd his cursed Steele away:

          Marke how the blood of Caesar followed it,

          As rushing out of doores, to be resolu'd

If Brutus so vnkindely knock'd, or no:

For Brutus, as you know, was Caesars Angel.

Iudge, O you Gods, how deerely Caesar lou'd him:

This was the most vnkindest cut of all.

For when the Noble Caesar saw him stab,

Ingratitude, more strong then Traitors armes,

Quite vanquish'd him: then burst his Mighty heart,

And in his Mantle, muffling vp his face

Euen at the Base of Pompeyes Statue

(Which all the while ran blood) great Caesar fell.

O what a fall was there, my Countrymen?Then

I, and you, and all of vs fell downe,

Whil'st bloody Treason flourish'd ouer vs.

O now you weepe, and I perceiue you feele

The dint of pitty: These are gracious droppes.

Kinde Soules, what weepe you, when you but behold

Our Caesars Vesture wounded? Looke you heere,

Heere is Himselfe, marr'd as you see with Traitors

1. O pitteous spectacle!

2. O Noble Caesar!

3. O wofull day!

4. O Traitors, Villaines!

1. O most bloody sight!

2. We will be reueng'd: Reuenge

About, seeke, burne, fire, kill, slay,

Let not a Traitor liue

Ant: Stay Country-men

1. Peace there, heare the Noble Antony

2. Wee'l heare him, wee'l follow him, wee'l dy with him

Ant: Good Friends, sweet Friends, let me not stirre
          you vp

          To such a sodaine Flood of Mutiny:

          They that haue done this Deede, are honoura-
          ble.

          What priuate greefes they haue, alas I know not,

          That made them do it: They are Wise, and Hon-
          ourable,

          And will no doubt with Reasons answer you.

          I come not (Friends) to steale away your hearts,

          I am no Orator, as Brutus is:

          But (as you know me all) a plaine blunt man

          That loue my Friend, and that they know full
          well,

          That gaue me publike leaue to speake of him:

          For I haue neyther writ nor words, nor worth,

Action, nor Vtterance, nor the power of Speech,

To stirre mens Blood. I onely speake right on:

I tell you that, which you your selues do know,

Shew you sweet Caesars wounds, poor poor dum mouths

And bid them speake for me: But were I Brutus,

And Brutus Antony, there were an Antony

Would ruffle vp your Spirits, and put a Tongue

In euery Wound of Caesar, that should moue

The stones of Rome, to rise and Mutiny

All: Wee'l Mutiny

1 Wee'l burne the house of Brutus

3 Away then, come, seeke the Conspirators

Ant: Yet heare me Countrymen, yet heare me speake

All: Peace hoe, heare Antony, most Noble Antony

Ant: Why Friends, you go to do you know not what:

         Wherein hath Caesar thus deseru'd your loues?

         Alas you know not, I must tell you then:

         You haue forgot the Will I told you of

All: Most true, the Will, let's stay and heare the Wil

Ant: Heere is the Will, and vnder Caesars Seale:

         To euery Roman Citizen he giues,

         To euery seuerall man, seuenty fiue Drachmaes

2 Ple: Most Noble Caesar, wee'l reuenge his death

3 Ple: O Royall Caesar

Ant: Heare me with patience

All: Peace hoe

Ant: Moreouer, he hath left you all his Walkes,

His priuate Arbors, and new-planted Orchards,

On this side Tyber, he hath left them you,

And to your heyres for euer: common pleasures

To walke abroad, and recreate your selues.

Heere was a Caesar: when comes such another?

1.Ple: Neuer, neuer: come, away, away:

Wee'l burne his body in the holy place,

And with the Brands fire the Traitors houses.

Take vp the body

2.Ple: Go fetch fire

3.Ple: Plucke downe Benches

4.Ple: Plucke downe Formes, Windowes, any thing.

Exit Plebeians.

Ant: Now let it worke: Mischeefe thou art a-foot,

Take thou what course thou wilt.

How now Fellow?

Enter Seruant.

Ser: Sir, Octauius is already come to Rome

Ant: Where is hee?

Ser: He and Lepidus are at Caesars house

Ant: And thither will I straight, to visit him:

He comes vpon a wish. Fortune is merry,

And in this mood will giue vs any thing

Ser: I heard him say, Brutus and Cassius

Are rid like Madmen through the Gates of Rome

Ant: Belike they had some notice of the people

How I had moued them. Bring me to Octauius.

Exeunt.

Enter Cinna the Poet, and after him the Plebeians.

Cinna: I dreamt to night, that I did feast with Caesar,

And things vnluckily charge my Fantasie:

I haue no will to wander foorth of doores,

Yet something leads me foorth

1. What is your name?

2. Whether are you going?

3. Where do you dwell?

4. Are you a married man, or a Batchellor?

2. Answer euery man directly

1. I, and breefely

4. I, and wisely

3. I, and truly, you were best

Cin: What is my name? Whether am I going? Where do I dwell? Am I a married man, or a Batchellour? Then to answer euery man, directly and breefely, wisely and truly: wisely I say, I am a Batchellor

      2 That's as much as to say, they are fooles that marrie: you'l beare me a bang for that I feare: proceede directly

Cinna: Directly I am going to Caesars Funerall

      1. As a Friend, or an Enemy? Cinna. As a friend

      2. That matter is answered directly

      4. For your dwelling: breefely

Cinna: Breefely, I dwell by the Capitoll

      3. Your name sir, truly

Cinna: Truly, my name is Cinna

      1. Teare him to peeces, hee's a Conspirator

Cinna: I am Cinna the Poet, I am Cinna the Poet

      4. Teare him for his bad verses, teare him for his bad Verses

Cin: I am not Cinna the Conspirator

      4. It is no matter, his name's Cinna, plucke but his name out of his heart, and turne him going

      3. Teare him, tear him; Come Brands hoe, Fire-brands: to Brutus, to Cassius, burne all. Some to Decius House, and some to Caska's; some to Ligarius: Away, go.

Exeunt. all the Plebeians.

Actus Quartus

Enter Antony, Octauius, and Lepidus.

Ant: These many then shall die, their names are prickt

Octa: Your Brother too must dye: consent you Lepi-dus?

Lep: I do consent

Octa: Pricke him downe Antony

Lep: Vpon condition Publius shall not liue,

Who is your Sisters sonne, Marke Antony

Ant: He shall not liue; looke, with a spot I dam him.

But Lepidus, go you to Caesars house:

Fetch the Will hither, and we shall determine

How to cut off some charge in Legacies

Lep: What? shall I finde you heere?

Octa: Or heere, or at the Capitoll.

Exit Lepidus

Ant: This is a slight vnmeritable man,

Meet to be sent on Errands: is it fit

The three-fold World diuided, he should stand

One of the three to share it?

Octa: So you thought him,

And tooke his voyce who should be prickt to dye

In our blacke Sentence and Proscription

Ant: Octauius, I haue seene more dayes then you,

And though we lay these Honours on this man,

To ease our selues of diuers sland'rous loads,

He shall but beare them, as the Asse beares Gold,

To groane and swet vnder the Businesse,

Either led or driuen, as we point the way:

And hauing brought our Treasure, where we will,

Then take we downe his Load, and turne him off

(Like to the empty Asse) to shake his eares,

And graze in Commons

Octa: You may do your will:

But hee's a tried, and valiant Souldier

Ant: So is my Horse Octauius, and for that

I do appoint him store of Prouender.

It is a Creature that I teach to fight,

To winde, to stop, to run directly on:

His corporall Motion, gouern'd by my Spirit,

And in some taste, is Lepidus but so:

He must be taught, and train'd, and bid go forth:

A barren spirited Fellow; one that feeds

On Obiects, Arts, and Imitations.

Which out of vse, and stal'de by other men

Begin his fashion. Do not talke of him,

But as a property: and now Octauius,

Listen great things. Brutus and Cassius

Are leuying Powers; We must straight make head:

Therefore let our Alliance be combin'd,

Our best Friends made, our meanes stretcht,

And let vs presently go sit in Councell,

How couert matters may be best disclos'd,

And open Perils surest answered

Octa: Let vs do so: for we are at the stake,

And bayed about with many Enemies,

And some that smile haue in their hearts I feare

Millions of Mischeefes.

Exeunt.

Drum. Enter Brutus, Lucillius, and the Army. Titinius and Pindarus meete them.

Bru: Stand ho

Lucil: Giue the word ho, and Stand

Bru: What now Lucillius, is Cassius neere?

Lucil: He is at hand, and Pindarus is come

To do you salutation from his Master

Bru: He greets me well. Your Master Pindarus

In his owne change, or by ill Officers,

Hath giuen me some worthy cause to wish

Things done, vndone: But if he be at hand

I shall be satisfied

Pin: I do not doubt

But that my Noble Master will appeare

Such as he is, full of regard, and Honour

Bru: He is not doubted. A word Lucillius

How he receiu'd you: let me be resolu'd

Lucil: With courtesie, and with respect enough,

But not with such familiar instances,

Nor with such free and friendly Conference

As he hath vs'd of old

Bru: Thou hast describ,d

A hot Friend, cooling: Euer note Lucillius,

When Loue begins to sicken and decay

It vseth an enforced Ceremony.

There are no trickes, in plaine and simple Faith:

But hollow men, like Horses hot at hand,

Make gallant shew, and promise of their Mettle:

Low March within.

But when they should endure the bloody Spurre,

They fall their Crests, and like deceitfull Iades

Sinke in the Triall. Comes his Army on?

Lucil: They meane this night in Sardis to be quarter'd:

The greater part, the Horse in generall

Are come with Cassius.

Enter Cassius and his Powers.

Bru: Hearke, he is arriu〉d:

    March gently on to meete him

Cassi: Stand ho

Bru: Stand ho, speake the word along.

    Stand.

    Stand.

    Stand

Cassi: Most Noble Brother, you haue done me wrong

Bru: Iudge me you Gods; wrong I mine Enemies?

    And if not so, how should I wrong a Brother

Cassi: Brutus, this sober forme of yours, hides wrongs,

    And when you do them-

Brut: Cassius, be content,

    Speake your greefes softly, I do know you well.

    Before the eyes of both our Armies heere

    (Which should perceiue nothing but Loue from
    vs)

    Let vs not wrangle. Bid them moue away:

    Then in my Tent Cassius enlarge your Greefes,

    And I will giue you Audience

Cassi: Pindarus,

    Bid our Commanders leade their Charges off

    A little from this ground

Bru: Lucillius, do you the like, and let no man

Come to our Tent, till we haue done our Conference.

Let Lucius and Titinius guard our doore.

Exeunt.

Manet Brutus and Cassius

Cassi: That you haue wrong‚d me, doth appear in this:
              You haue condemn'd, and noted Lucius Pella
              For taking Bribes heere of the Sardians;
              Wherein my Letters, praying on his side,
              Because I knew the man was slighted off

Bru: You wrong'd your selfe to write in such a case

Cassi: In such a time as this, it is not meet
              That euery nice offence should beare his Comment

Bru: Let me tell you Cassius, you your selfe
              Are much condemn'd to haue an itching Palme,
              To sell, and Mart your Offices for Gold
              To Vndeseruers

Cassi: I, an itching Palme?
              You know that you are Brutus that speakes this,
              Or by the Gods, this speech were else your last

Bru: The name of Cassius Honors this corruption,
              And Chasticement doth therefore hide his head

Cassi: Chasticement?

Bru: Remember March, the Ides of March reme[m]
              ber:

Did not great Iulius bleede for Iustice sake?

What Villaine touch'd his body, that did stab,

And not for Iustice? What? Shall one of Vs,

That strucke the Formost man of all this World,

But for supporting Robbers: shall we now,

Contaminate our fingers, with base Bribes?

And sell the mighty space of our large Honors

For so much trash, as may be grasped thus?

I had rather be a Dogge, and bay the Moone,

Then such a Roman

Cassi: Brutus, baite not me,

Ile not indure it: you forget your selfe

To hedge me in. I am a Souldier, I,

Older in practice, Abler then your selfe

To make Conditions

Bru: Go too: you are not Cassius

Cassi: I am

Bru: I say, you are not

Cassi: Vrge me no more, I shall forget my selfe:

Haue minde vpon your health: Tempt me no far-
ther

Bru: Away slight man

Cassi: Is't possible?

Bru: Heare me, for I will speake.

Must I giue way, and roome to your rash Chol-
ler?

	Shall I be frighted, when a Madman stares?
Cassi:	O ye Gods, ye Gods, Must I endure all this?
Bru:	All this? I more: Fret till your proud hart break.
	Go shew your Slaues how Chollericke you are,
	And make your Bondmen tremble. Must I bouge?
	Must I obserue you? Must I stand and crouch
	Vnder your Testie Humour? By the Gods,
	You shall digest the Venom of your Spleene
	Though it do Split you. For, from this day forth,
	Ile vse you for my Mirth, yea for my Laughter
	When you are Waspish
Cassi:	Is it come to this?
Bru:	You say, you are a better Souldier:
	Let it appeare so; make your vaunting true,
	And it shall please me well. For mine owne part,
	I shall be glad to learne of Noble men
Cass:	You wrong me euery way:
	You wrong me Brutus:
	I saide, an Elder Souldier, not a Better.
	Did I say Better?
Bru:	If you did, I care not
Cass:	When Caesar liu'd, he durst not thus haue mou'd me
Brut:	Peace, peace, you durst not so haue tempted him
Cassi:	I durst not

Bru: No

Cassi: What? durst not tempt him?

Bru: For your life you durst not

Cassi: Do not presume too much vpon my Loue,

I may do that I shall be sorry for

Bru: You haue done that you should be sorry for.

There is no terror Cassius in your threats:

For I am Arm'd so strong in Honesty,

That they passe by me, as the idle winde,

Which I respect not. I did send to you

For certaine summes of Gold, which you deny'd
me,

For I can raise no money by vile meanes:

By Heauen, I had rather Coine my Heart,

And drop my blood for Drachmaes, then to
wring

From the hard hands of Peazants, their vile
trash

By any indirection. I did send

To you for Gold to pay my Legions,

Which you deny'd me: was that done like Cassius?

Should I haue answer'd Caius Cassius so?

When Marcus Brutus growes so Couetous,

To locke such Rascall Counters from his Friends,

Be ready Gods with all your Thunder-bolts,

	Dash him to peeces
Cassi:	I deny'd you not
Bru:	You did
Cassi:	I did not. He was but a Foole

That brought my answer back. Brutus hath riu'd my hart:

A Friend should beare his Friends infirmities;

But Brutus makes mine greater then they are

Bru:	I do not, till you practice them on me
Cassi:	You loue me not
Bru:	I do not like your faults
Cassi:	A friendly eye could neuer see such faults
Bru:	A Flatterers would not, though they do appeare

As huge as high Olympus

Cassi: Come Antony, and yong Octauius come,

Reuenge your selues alone on Cassius,

For Cassius is a-weary of the World:

Hated by one he loues, brau'd by his Brother,

Check'd like a bondman, all his faults obseru'd,

Set in a Note-booke, learn'd, and con'd by roate

To cast into my Teeth. O I could weepe

My Spirit from mine eyes. There is my Dagger,

And heere my naked Breast: Within, a Heart

Deerer then Pluto's Mine, Richer then Gold:

If that thou bee'st a Roman, take it foorth.

I that deny'd thee Gold, will giue my Heart:

Strike as thou did'st at Caesar: For I know,

When thou did'st hate him worst, y loued'st him better

Then euer thou loued'st Cassius

Bru: Sheath your Dagger:

Be angry when you will, it shall haue scope:

Do what you will, Dishonor, shall be Humour.

O Cassius, you are yoaked with a Lambe

That carries Anger, as the Flint beares fire,

Who much inforced, shewes a hastie Sparke,

And straite is cold agen

Cassi: Hath Cassius liu›d

To be but Mirth and Laughter to his Brutus,

When greefe and blood ill temper'd, vexeth him?

Bru: When I spoke that, I was ill temper'd too

Cassi: Do you confesse so much? Giue me your hand

Bru: And my heart too

Cassi: O Brutus!

Bru: What's the matter?

Cassi: Haue not you loue enough to beare with me,

When that rash humour which my Mother gaue me

Makes me forgetfull

Bru: Yes Cassius, and from henceforth

When you are ouer-earnest with your Brutus,

Hee'l thinke your Mother chides, and leaue you so.

Enter a Poet.

Poet: Let me go in to see the Generals,

There is some grudge betweene 'em, 'tis not meete

They be alone

Lucil: You shall not come to them

Poet: Nothing but death shall stay me

Cas: How now? What›s the matter?

Poet: For shame you Generals; what do you meane?

Loue, and be Friends, as two such men should bee,

For I haue seene more yeeres I'me sure then yee

Cas: Ha, ha, how vildely doth this Cynicke rime?

Bru: Get you hence sirra: Sawcy Fellow, hence

Cas: Beare with him Brutus, 'tis his fashion

Brut: Ile know his humor, when he knowes his time:

What should the Warres do with these Iigging Fooles?

Companion, hence

Cas: Away, away be gone.

Exit Poet

Bru: Lucillius and Titinius bid the Commanders

Prepare to lodge their Companies to night

Cas: And come your selues, & bring Messala with you
        Immediately to vs

Bru: Lucius, a bowle of Wine

Cas: I did not thinke you could haue bin so angry

Bru: O Cassius, I am sicke of many greefes

Cas: Of your Philosophy you make no vse,
        If you giue place to accidentall euils

Bru: No man beares sorrow better. Portia is dead

Cas: Ha? Portia?

Bru: She is dead

Cas: How scap›d I killing, when I crost you so?
        O insupportable, and touching losse!
        Vpon what sicknesse?

Bru: Impatient of my absence,
        And greefe, that yong Octauius with Mark An-
        tony
        Haue made themselues so strong: For with her
        death
        That tydings came. With this she fell distract,
        And (her Attendants absent) swallow'd fire

Cas: And dy›d so?

Bru: Euen so

Cas: O ye immortall Gods!

Enter Boy with Wine, and Tapers.

Bru: Speak no more of her: Giue me a bowl of wine,

In this I bury all vnkindnesse Cassius.

Drinkes

Cas: My heart is thirsty for that Noble pledge.

Fill Lucius, till the Wine ore-swell the Cup:

I cannot drinke too much of Brutus loue.

Enter Titinius and Messala.

Brutus: Come in Titinius:

Welcome good Messala:

Now sit we close about this Taper heere,

And call in question our necessities

Cass: Portia, art thou gone?

Bru: No more I pray you.

Messala, I haue heere receiued Letters,

That yong Octauius, and Marke Antony

Come downe vpon vs with a mighty power,

Bending their Expedition toward Philippi

Mess: My selfe haue Letters of the selfe-same Tenure

Bru: With what Addition

Mess: That by proscription, and billes of Outlarie,

Octauius, Antony, and Lepidus,

Haue put to death, an hundred Senators

Bru: Therein our Letters do not well agree:

Mine speake of seuenty Senators, that dy'de

By their proscriptions, Cicero being one

Cassi: Cicero one?

Messa: Cicero is dead, and by that order of proscription

        Had you your Letters from your wife, my Lord?

Bru: No Messala

Messa: Nor nothing in your Letters writ of her?

Bru: Nothing Messala

Messa: That me thinkes is strange

Bru: Why aske you?

        Heare you ought of her, in yours?

Messa: No my Lord

Bru: Now as you are a Roman tell me true

Messa: Then like a Roman, beare the truth I tell,

        For certaine she is dead, and by strange manner

Bru: Why farewell Portia: We must die Messala:

        With meditating that she must dye once,

        I haue the patience to endure it now

Messa: Euen so great men, great losses shold indure

Cassi: I haue as much of this in Art as you,

        But yet my Nature could not beare it so

Bru: Well, to our worke aliue. What do you thinke

        Of marching to Philippi presently

Cassi: I do not thinke it good

Bru: Your reason?

Cassi: This it is:

        'Tis better that the Enemie seeke vs,

So shall he waste his meanes, weary his Sould-

iers,

Doing himselfe offence, whil'st we lying still,

Are full of rest, defence, and nimblenesse

Bru: Good reasons must of force giue place to better:

The people 'twixt Philippi, and this ground

Do stand but in a forc'd affection:

For they haue grug'd vs Contribution.

The Enemy, marching along by them,

By them shall make a fuller number vp,

Come on refresht, new added, and encourag'd:

From which aduantage shall we cut him off.

If at Philippi we do face him there,

These people at our backe

Cassi: Heare me good Brother

Bru: Vnder your pardon. You must note beside,

That we haue tride the vtmost of our Friends:

Our Legions are brim full, our cause is ripe,

The Enemy encreaseth euery day,

We at the height, are readie to decline.

There is a Tide in the affayres of men,

Which taken at the Flood, leades on to Fortune:

Omitted, all the voyage of their life,

Is bound in Shallowes, and in Miseries.

On such a full Sea are we now a-float,

> And we must take the current when it serues,
> Or loose our Ventures

Cassi: Then with your will go on: wee›l along
> Our selues, and meet them at Philippi

Bru: The deepe of night is crept vpon our talke,
> And Nature must obey Necessitie,
> Which we will niggard with a little rest:
> There is no more to say

Cassi: No more, good night,
> Early to morrow will we rise, and hence.

Enter Lucius.

Bru: Lucius my Gowne: farewell good Messala,
> Good night Titinius: Noble, Noble Cassius,
> Good night, and good repose

Cassi: O my deere Brother:
> This was an ill beginning of the night:
> Neuer come such diuision 'tweene our soules:
> Let it not Brutus.

Enter Lucius with the Gowne.

Bru: Euery thing is well

Cassi: Good night my Lord

Bru: Good night good Brother

Tit: Messa. Good night Lord Brutus

Bru: Farwell euery one.

Exeunt.

Giue me the Gowne. Where is thy Instrument?

Luc: Heere in the Tent

Bru: What, thou speak>st drowsily?

         Poore knaue I blame thee not, thou art ore-
watch'd.

         Call Claudio, and some other of my men,

         Ile haue them sleepe on Cushions in my Tent

Luc: Varrus, and Claudio.

Enter Varrus and Claudio.

Var: Cals my Lord?

Bru: I pray you sirs, lye in my Tent and sleepe,

         It may be I shall raise you by and by

         On businesse to my Brother Cassius

Var: So please you, we will stand,

         And watch your pleasure

Bru: I will it not haue it so: Lye downe good sirs,

         It may be I shall otherwise bethinke me.

         Looke Lucius, heere's the booke I sought for so:

         I put it in the pocket of my Gowne

Luc: I was sure your Lordship did not giue it me

Bru: Beare with me good Boy, I am much forgetfull.

         Canst thou hold vp thy heauie eyes a-while,

         And touch thy Instrument a straine or two

Luc: I my Lord, an't please you

Bru: It does my Boy:

        I trouble thee too much, but thou art willing

Luc: It is my duty Sir

Brut: I should not vrge thy duty past thy might,

        I know yong bloods looke for a time of rest

Luc: I haue slept my Lord already

Bru: It was well done, and thou shalt sleepe againe:

        I will not hold thee long. If I do liue,

        I will be good to thee.

Musicke, and a Song.

This is a sleepy Tune: O Murd'rous slumber!

Layest thou thy Leaden Mace vpon my Boy,

That playes thee Musicke? Gentle knaue good night:

I will not do thee so much wrong to wake thee:

If thou do'st nod, thou break'st thy Instrument,

Ile take it from thee, and (good Boy) good night.

Let me see, let me see; is not the Leafe turn'd downe

Where I left reading? Heere it is I thinke.

Enter the Ghost of Caesar.

How ill this Taper burnes. Ha! Who comes heere?

I thinke it is the weakenesse of mine eyes

That shapes this monstrous Apparition.

It comes vpon me: Art thou any thing?

Art thou some God, some Angell, or some Diuell,

That mak'st my blood cold, and my haire to stare?

Speake to me, what thou art

Ghost:	Thy euill Spirit Brutus?
Bru:	Why com'st thou?
Ghost:	To tell thee thou shalt see me at Philippi
Brut:	Well: then I shall see thee againe?
Ghost:	I, at Philippi
Brut:	Why I will see thee at Philippi then:
	Now I haue taken heart, thou vanishest.
	Ill Spirit, I would hold more talke with thee.
	Boy, Lucius, Varrus, Claudio, Sirs: Awake: Claudio
Luc:	The strings my Lord, are false
Bru:	He thinkes he still is at his Instrument. Lucius, awake
Luc:	My Lord
Bru:	Did'st thou dreame Lucius, that thou so cryedst out?
Luc:	My Lord, I do not know that I did cry
Bru:	Yes that thou did'st: Did'st thou see any thing?
Luc:	Nothing my Lord
Bru:	Sleepe againe Lucius: Sirra Claudio, Fellow, Thou: Awake
Var:	My Lord
Clau:	My Lord

Bru: Why did you so cry out sirs, in your sleepe?

Both: Did we my Lord?

Bru: I: saw you any thing?

Var: No my Lord, I saw nothing

Clau: Nor I my Lord

Bru: Go, and commend me to my Brother Cassius:

        Bid him set on his Powres betimes before,

        And we will follow

Both: It shall be done my Lord.

Exeunt.

Actus Quintus

Enter Octauius, Antony, and their Army.

Octa: Now Antony, our hopes are answered,
            You said the Enemy would not come downe,
            But keepe the Hilles and vpper Regions:
            It proues not so: their battailes are at hand,
            They meane to warne vs at Philippi heere:
            Answering before we do demand of them
Ant: Tut I am in their bosomes, and I know
            Wherefore they do it: They could be content
            To visit other places, and come downe
            With fearefull brauery: thinking by this face
            To fasten in our thoughts that they haue Cour-
            age;
            But 'tis not so.

Enter a Messenger.

Mes: Prepare you Generals,
            The Enemy comes on in gallant shew:
            Their bloody signe of Battell is hung out,
            And something to be done immediately

Ant: Octauius, leade your Battaile softly on Vpon the
          left hand of the euen Field

Octa: Vpon the right hand I, keepe thou the left

Ant: Why do you crosse me in this exigent

Octa: I do not crosse you: but I will do so.

          March.

Drum. Enter Brutus, Cassius, & their Army.

Bru: They stand, and would haue parley

Cassi: Stand fast Titinius, we must out and talke

Octa: Mark Antony, shall we giue signe of Battaile?

Ant: No Caesar, we will answer on their Charge.

          Make forth, the Generals would haue some
          words

Oct: Stirre not vntill the Signall

Bru: Words before blowes: is it so Countrymen?

Octa: Not that we loue words better, as you do

Bru: Good words are better then bad strokes Octaui-
          us

An: In your bad strokes Brutus, you giue good words

          Witnesse the hole you made in Caesars heart,

          Crying long liue, Haile Caesar

Cassi: Antony,

          The posture of your blowes are yet vnknowne;

          But for your words, they rob the Hibla Bees,

          And leaue them Hony-lesse

Ant: Not stinglesse too

Bru: O yes, and soundlesse too:

          For you haue stolne their buzzing Antony,

          And very wisely threat before you sting

Ant: Villains: you did not so, when your vile daggers

          Hackt one another in the sides of Caesar:

          You shew'd your teethes like Apes,

          And fawn'd like Hounds,

          And bow'd like Bondmen, kissing Caesars feete;

          Whil'st damned Caska, like a Curre, behinde

          Strooke Caesar on the necke. O you Flatterers

Cassi: Flatterers? Now Brutus thanke your selfe,

          This tongue had not offended so to day.

          If Cassius might haue rul'd

Octa: Come, come, the cause. If arguing make vs swet,

          The proofe of it will turne to redder drops:

          Looke, I draw a Sword against Conspirators,

          When thinke you that the Sword goes vp againe?

          Neuer till Caesars three and thirtie wounds

          Be well aueng'd; or till another Caesar

          Haue added slaughter to the Sword of Traitors

Brut: Caesar, thou canst not dye by Traitors hands.

          Vnlesse thou bring'st them with thee

Octa: So I hope:

          I was not borne to dye on Brutus Sword

Bru: O if thou wer>t the Noblest of thy Straine,

Yong-man, thou could'st not dye more honour-able

Cassi: A peeuish School-boy, worthles of such Honor
Ioyn'd with a Masker, and a Reueller

Ant: Old Cassius still

Octa: Come Antony: away:

Defiance Traitors, hurle we in your teeth.

If you dare fight to day, come to the Field;

If not, when you haue stomackes.

Exit Octauius, Antony, and Army

Cassi: Why now blow winde, swell Billow,

And swimme Barke:

The Storme is vp, and all is on the hazard

Bru: Ho Lucillius, hearke, a word with you.

Lucillius and Messala stand forth.

Luc: My Lord

Cassi: Messala

Messa: What sayes my Generall?

Cassi: Messala, this is my Birth-day: at this very day

Was Cassius borne. Giue me thy hand Messala:

Be thou my witnesse, that against my will

(As Pompey was) am I compell'd to set

Vpon one Battell all our Liberties.

You know, that I held Epicurus strong,

And his Opinion: Now I change my minde,

And partly credit things that do presage.

Comming from Sardis, on our former Ensigne

Two mighty Eagles fell, and there they pearch'd,

Gorging and feeding from our Soldiers hands,

Who to Philippi heere consorted vs:

This Morning are they fled away, and gone,

And in their steeds, do Rauens, Crowes, and Kites

Fly ore our heads, and downward looke on vs

As we were sickely prey; their shadowes seeme

A Canopy most fatall, vnder which

Our Army lies, ready to giue vp the Ghost

Messa: Beleeue not so

Cassi: I but beleeue it partly,

For I am fresh of spirit, and resolu'd

To meete all perils, very constantly

Bru: Euen so Lucillius

Cassi: Now most Noble Brutus,

The Gods to day stand friendly, that we may

Louers in peace, leade on our dayes to age.

But since the affayres of men rests still incertaine,

Let's reason with the worst that may befall.

If we do lose this Battaile, then is this

The very last time we shall speake together:

What are you then determined to do?

Bru: Euen by the rule of that Philosophy,

By which I did blame Cato, for the death

Which he did giue himselfe, I know not how:

But I do finde it Cowardly, and vile,

For feare of what might fall, so to preuent

The time of life, arming my selfe with patience,

To stay the prouidence of some high Powers,

That gouerne vs below

Cassi: Then, if we loose this Battaile,

You are contented to be led in Triumph

Thorow the streets of Rome

Bru: No Cassius, no:

Thinke not thou Noble Romane,

That euer Brutus will go bound to Rome,

He beares too great a minde. But this same day

Must end that worke, the Ides of March begun.

And whether we shall meete againe, I know not:

Therefore our euerlasting farewell take:

For euer, and for euer, farewell Cassius,

If we do meete againe, why we shall smile;

If not, why then this parting was well made

Cassi: For euer, and for euer, farewell Brutus:

If we do meete againe, wee'l smile indeede;

If not, 'tis true, this parting was well made

Bru: Why then leade on. O that a man might know
        The end of this dayes businesse, ere it come:
        But it sufficeth, that the day will end,
        And then the end is knowne. Come ho, away.

Exeunt.

Alarum. Enter Brutus and Messala.

Bru: Ride, ride Messala, ride and giue these Billes
        Vnto the Legions, on the other side.

Lowd Alarum.

Let them set on at once: for I perceiue

But cold demeanor in Octauio's wing:

And sodaine push giues them the ouerthrow:

Ride, ride Messala, let them all come downe.

Exeunt.

Alarums. Enter Cassius and Titinius.

Cassi: O looke Titinius, looke, the Villaines flye:
        My selfe haue to mine owne turn'd Enemy:
        This Ensigne heere of mine was turning backe,
        I slew the Coward, and did take it from him

Titin: O Cassius, Brutus gaue the word too early,
        Who hauing some aduantage on Octauius,
        Tooke it too eagerly: his Soldiers fell to spoyle,
        Whilst we by Antony are all inclos'd.

Enter Pindarus.

Pind: Fly further off my Lord: flye further off,

        Mark Antony is in your Tents my Lord:

        Flye therefore Noble Cassius, flye farre off

Cassi: This Hill is farre enough. Looke, look Titinius

        Are those my Tents where I perceiue the fire?

Tit: They are, my Lord

Cassi: Titinius, if thou louest me,

        Mount thou my horse, and hide thy spurres in
        him,

        Till he haue brought thee vp to yonder Troopes

        And heere againe, that I may rest assur'd

        Whether yond Troopes, are Friend or Enemy

Tit: I will be heere againe, euen with a thought.

Enter.

Cassi: Go Pindarus, get higher on that hill,

        My sight was euer thicke: regard Titinius,

        And tell me what thou not'st about the Field.

        This day I breathed first, Time is come round,

        And where I did begin, there shall I end,

        My life is run his compasse. Sirra, what newes?

Pind: Aboue. O my Lord

Cassi: What newes?

Pind: Titinius is enclosed round about

        With Horsemen, that make to him on the Spurre,

Yet he spurres on. Now they are almost on him:

Now Titinius. Now some light: O he lights too.

Hee's tane.

Showt.

And hearke, they shout for ioy

Cassi: Come downe, behold no more:

        O Coward that I am, to liue so long,

        To see my best Friend tane before my face

Enter Pindarus.

Come hither sirrah: In Parthia did I take thee Prisoner,

And then I swore thee, sauing of thy life,

That whatsoeuer I did bid thee do,

Thou should'st attempt it. Come now, keepe thine oath,

Now be a Free-man, and with this good Sword

That ran through Caesars bowels, search this bosome.

Stand not to answer: Heere, take thou the Hilts,

And when my face is couer'd, as 'tis now,

Guide thou the Sword- Caesar, thou art reueng'd,

Euen with the Sword that kill'd thee

Pin: So, I am free,

        Yet would not so haue beene

        Durst I haue done my will. O Cassius,

        Farre from this Country Pindarus shall run,

        Where neuer Roman shall take note of him.

Enter Titinius and Messala.

Messa:	It is but change, Titinius: for Octauius
	Is ouerthrowne by Noble Brutus power,
	As Cassius Legions are by Antony
Titin:	These tydings will well comfort Cassius
Messa:	Where did you leaue him
Titin:	All disconsolate,
	With Pindarus his Bondman, on this Hill
Messa:	Is not that he that lyes vpon the ground?
Titin:	He lies not like the Liuing. O my heart!
Messa:	Is not that hee?
Titin:	No, this was he Messala,
	But Cassius is no more. O setting Sunne:
	As in thy red Rayes thou doest sinke to night;
	So in his red blood Cassius day is set.
	The Sunne of Rome is set. Our day is gone,
	Clowds, Dewes, and Dangers come; our deeds are done:
	Mistrust of my successe hath done this deed
Messa:	Mistrust of good successe hath done this deed.
	O hatefull Error, Melancholies Childe:
	Why do'st thou shew to the apt thoughts of men
	The things that are not? O Error soone con-ceyu'd,
	Thou neuer com'st vnto a happy byrth,

	But kil'st the Mother that engendred thee
Tit:	What Pindarus? Where art thou Pindarus?
Messa:	Seeke him Titinius, whilst I go to meet
	The Noble Brutus, thrusting this report
	Into his eares; I may say thrusting it:
	For piercing Steele, and Darts inuenomed,
	Shall be as welcome to the eares of Brutus,
	As tydings of this sight
Tit:	Hye you Messala,

And I will seeke for Pindarus the while:

Why did'st thou send me forth braue Cassius?

Did I not meet thy Friends, and did not they

Put on my Browes this wreath of Victorie,

And bid me giue it thee? Did'st thou not heare their showts?

Alas, thou hast misconstrued euery thing.

But hold thee, take this Garland on thy Brow,

Thy Brutus bid me giue it thee, and I

Will do his bidding. Brutus, come apace,

And see how I regarded Caius Cassius:

By your leaue Gods: This is a Romans part,

Come Cassius Sword, and finde Titinius hart.

Dies

Alarum. Enter Brutus, Messala, yong Cato, Strato, Volumnius, and Lucillius.

Bru:	Where, where Messala, doth his body lye?
Messa:	Loe yonder, and Titinius mourning it
Bru:	Titinius face is vpward
Cato:	He is slaine
Bru:	O Iulius Caesar, thou art mighty yet,
	Thy Spirit walkes abroad, and turnes our Swords
	In our owne proper Entrailes. Low Alarums
Cato:	Braue Titinius,
	Looke where he haue not crown'd dead Cassius
Bru:	Are yet two Romans liuing such as these?
	The last of all the Romans, far thee well:
	It is impossible, that euer Rome
	Should breed thy fellow. Friends I owe mo teares
	To this dead man, then you shall see me pay.
	I shall finde time, Cassius: I shall finde time.
	Come therefore, and to Tharsus send his body,
	His Funerals shall not be in our Campe,
	Least it discomfort vs. Lucillius come,
	And come yong Cato, let vs to the Field,
	Labio and Flauio set our Battailes on:
	'Tis three a clocke, and Romans yet ere night,
	We shall try Fortune in a second fight.

Exeunt.

Alarum. Enter Brutus, Messala, Cato, Lucillius, and Flauius.

Bru: Yet Country-men: O yet, hold vp your heads

Cato: What Bastard doth not? Who will go with me?

I will proclaime my name about the Field.

I am the Sonne of Marcus Cato, hoe.

A Foe to Tyrants, and my Countries Friend.

I am the Sonne of Marcus Cato, hoe.

Enter Souldiers, and fight.

And I am Brutus, Marcus Brutus, I,

Brutus my Countries Friend: Know me for Brutus

Luc: O yong and Noble Cato, art thou downe?

Why now thou dyest, as brauely as Titinius,

And may'st be honour'd, being Cato's Sonne

Sold: Yeeld, or thou dyest

Luc: Onely I yeeld to dye:

There is so much, that thou wilt kill me straight:

Kill Brutus, and be honour'd in his death

Sold: We must not: a Noble Prisoner.

Enter Antony.

2. Sold: Roome hoe: tell Antony, Brutus is tane

1. Sold: Ile tell thee newes. Heere comes the Generall,

Brutus is tane, Brutus is tane my Lord

Ant: Where is hee?

Luc:	Safe Antony, Brutus is safe enough:
	I dare assure thee, that no Enemy
	Shall euer take aliue the Noble Brutus:
	The Gods defend him from so great a shame,
	When you do finde him, or aliue, or dead,
	He will be found like Brutus, like himselfe
Ant:	This is not Brutus friend, but I assure you,
	A prize no lesse in worth; keepe this man safe,
	Giue him all kindnesse. I had rather haue
	Such men my Friends, then Enemies. Go on,
	And see where Brutus be aliue or dead,
	And bring vs word, vnto Octauius Tent:
	How euery thing is chanc'd.

Exeunt.

Enter Brutus, Dardanius, Clitus, Strato, and Volum-nius.

Brut:	Come poore remaines of friends, rest on this Rocke
Clit:	Statillius shew)d the Torch-light, but my Lord He came not backe: he is or tane, or slaine
Brut:	Sit thee downe, Clitus: slaying is the word, It is a deed in fashion. Hearke thee, Clitus
Clit:	What I, my Lord? No, not for all the World
Brut:	Peace then, no words

Clit:	Ile rather kill my selfe
Brut:	Hearke thee, Dardanius
Dard:	Shall I doe such a deed?
Clit:	O Dardanius
Dard:	O Clitus
Clit:	What ill request did Brutus make to thee?
Dard:	To kill him, Clitus: looke he meditates
Clit:	Now is that Noble Vessell full of griefe,
	That it runnes ouer euen at his eyes
Brut:	Come hither, good Volumnius, list a word
Volum:	What sayes my Lord?
Brut:	Why this, Volumnius:
	The Ghost of Caesar hath appear'd to me
	Two seuerall times by Night: at Sardis, once;
	And this last Night, here in Philippi fields:
	I know my houre is come
Volum:	Not so, my Lord
Brut:	Nay, I am sure it is, Volumnius.
	Thou seest the World, Volumnius, how it goes,
	Our Enemies haue beat vs to the Pit:

Low Alarums.

It is more worthy, to leape in our selues,

Then tarry till they push vs. Good Volumnius,

Thou know'st, that we two went to Schoole together:

Euen for that our loue of old, I prethee

Hold thou my Sword Hilts, whilest I runne on it

Vol: That's not an Office for a friend, my Lord.

Alarum still.

Cly: Fly, flye my Lord, there is no tarrying heere

Bru: Farewell to you, and you, and Volumnius.

            Strato, thou hast bin all this while asleepe:

            Farewell to thee, to Strato, Countrymen:

            My heart doth ioy, that yet in all my life,

            I found no man, but he was true to me.

            I shall haue glory by this loosing day

            More then Octauius, and Marke Antony,

            By this vile Conquest shall attaine vnto.

            So fare you well at once, for Brutus tongue

            Hath almost ended his liues History:

            Night hangs vpon mine eyes, my Bones would rest,

            That haue but labour'd, to attaine this houre.

Alarum: Cry within, Flye, flye, flye.

Cly: Fly my Lord, flye

Bru: Hence: I will follow:

            I prythee Strato, stay thou by thy Lord,

            Thou art a Fellow of a good respect:

            Thy life hath had some smatch of Honor in it,

            Hold then my Sword, and turne away thy face,

While I do run vpon it. Wilt thou Strato?

Stra: Giue me your hand first. Fare you wel my Lord

Bru: Farewell good Strato. - Caesar, now be still,

I kill'd not thee with halfe so good a will. *Dyes.*

Alarum. Retreat.

Enter Antony, O tauius, Messala, Lucillius, and the Army.

Octa: What man is that?

Messa: My Masters man. Strato, where is thy Master?

Stra: Free from the Bondage you are in Messala,

The Conquerors can but make a fire of him:

For Brutus onely ouercame himselfe,

And no man else hath Honor by his death

Lucil: So Brutus should be found. I thank thee Brutus

That thou hast prou'd Lucillius saying true,

Octa: All that seru·d Brutus, I will entertaine them.

Fellow, wilt thou bestow thy time with me?

Stra: I, if Messala will preferre me to you

Octa: Do so, good Messala

Messa: How dyed my Master Strato?

Stra: I held the Sword, and he did run on it

Messa: Octauius, then take him to follow thee,

That did the latest seruice to my Master

Ant: This was the Noblest Roman of them all:

All the Conspirators saue onely hee,

Did that they did, in enuy of great Caesar:

He, onely in a generall honest thought,

And common good to all, made one of them.

His life was gentle, and the Elements

So mixt in him, that Nature might stand vp,

And say to all the world; This was a man

Octa: According to his Vertue, let vs vse him

Withall Respect, and Rites of Buriall.

Within my Tent his bones to night shall ly,

Most like a Souldier ordered Honourably:

So call the Field to rest, and let's away,

To part the glories of this happy day.

Exeunt. omnes.

Made in the USA
Monee, IL
07 July 2026

56552348R00080